LEEDS METROPOLITAN UNIVERSITY

MANAGING EXTERNAL RELATIONS

Managing Universities and Colleges: Guides to Good Practice

Series editors:

David Warner, Principal and Chief Executive, Swansea Institute of Higher Education

David Palfreyman, Bursar and Fellow, New College, Oxford

This series has been commissioned in order to provide systematic analysis of the major areas of the management of colleges and universities, emphasizing good practice.

Current titles:

Frank Albrighton and Julia Thomas (eds): *Managing External Relations*
Allan Bolton: *Managing the Academic Unit*
Ann Edworthy: *Managing Stress*
Judith Elkin and Derek Law (eds): *Managing Information*
John M. Gledhill: *Managing Students*
Christine Humfrey: *Managing International Students*
Colleen Liston: *Managing Quality and Standards*
David Watson: *Managing Strategy*

MANAGING EXTERNAL RELATIONS

Edited by
**Frank Albrighton and
Julia Thomas**

Open University Press
Buckingham · Philadelphia

Open University Press
Celtic Court
22 Ballmoor
Buckingham
MK18 1XW

email: enquiries@openup.co.uk
world wide web: www.openup.co.uk

and

325 Chestnut Street
Philadelphia, PA 19106, USA

First Published 2001

A catalogue record of this book is available from the British Library

ISBN   0 335 20789 8 (pb)   0 335 20790 1 (hb)

Library of Congress Cataloging-in-Publication Data
Managing external relations / [edited by] Frank Albrighton and
Julia Thomas.
    p.   cm. – (Managing universities and colleges)
   Includes bibliographical references and index.
   ISBN 0-335-20790-1 – ISBN 0-335-20789-8 (pbk.)
   1. Universities and colleges–Public relations   I. Albrighton, Frank, 1944–
II. Thomas, Julia, 1947–   III. Series.

LB2342.8.M36   2001
659.2′9378–dc21

                                                                00-065249

Typeset by Graphicraft Limited, Hong Kong
Printed in Great Britain by The Cromwell Press, Trowbridge

CONTENTS

Series editors' introduction   ix
List of figures and tables   xiii
Preface   xv
Notes on contributors   xvii

1   What is external relations for?   **1**

Frank Albrighton and Julia Thomas

2   A rose by any other name
Brand management and visual identity   **8**

Frank Albrighton and Julia Thomas

3   So that's what they think
Market research   **20**

Roger Stubbs

The role of opinion research   20
Examples of higher education research   21
How does market research work?   22
How to gather the information   23
Qualitative research   24
How to choose   26

Whom to survey? The principles of sampling 27
Formulating the questions to ask 30
Market research 'deliverables' 31
Cost-effectiveness of market research 31
Further reading 32

4 Impress in print
Publications

33

Frank Albrighton and Julia Thomas

Who is in charge? 38
Who is going to write it? 39
Design: I know what I like 40
Who shall we get to print it? 42

5 Commercial breaks
A planned approach to advertising

44

Cyrrhian Macrae

Effective advertising 46
The role of research 47
How to plan a campaign 49
Setting your budget 51
Achieving value for money 52
A uniform approach 53
Conclusion 53

6 Casting your net
The Internet and its role in education marketing

55

Michael Stoner

Thinking across media 55
Promoting a culture of change 57
Developing a website that markets the institution
effectively 59
Other applications for the web: business processes
and learning and teaching 60

7   **'Happy Days' or 'Nightmare on Fleet Street'?**
     Media relations   66

     Peter Evans

     Uncertainties of the marketplace   67
     What the interviewer really wants   68
     Preparing for interviews   69
     Selecting your material   70
     Common problems   71
     The importance of pictures   72
     Can things go wrong?   74
     Editors' note   75
     Further reading   75

8   **Why aren't we speaking to each other?**
     Internal communications   76

     Frank Albrighton and Julia Thomas

9   **Guess who's coming to dinner!**
     Event management   87

     Frank Albrighton and Julia Thomas

10   **What are friends for?**
     Alumni relations   97

     Reggie Simpson

     Organizational and budgetary considerations   99
     Building a programme   100
     When does it all begin?   106
     Future trends and scenarios   107
     Alumni and development   107

11   **Money, money, money**
     Managing the fundraising process   108

     Elizabeth Smith

     The fundraising process   109

12 Well connected
Organizational structure

121

Frank Albrighton and Julia Thomas

13 All together now
A strategic institutional approach to integrated marketing

129

Larry D. Lauer

Why now? 129
How does integrated marketing relate to higher education? 130
Developing a model at Texas Christian University 131
Transforming institutions 131
Marketing higher education as a way of thinking 132
Integrated marketing communications 134
Branding 135
New focus on research 136
Launching integrated marketing 137
Integrated marketing and student recruiting 138
Lessons about visibility 138
Lessons for alumni and development programmes 140
Integrated marketing and strategic planning 140
Integrated marketing and the future of higher education 141
Further reading 141

14 A seat at the table
Performance measurement

143

James Mahoney

Appendix 157
Index 161

SERIES EDITORS' INTRODUCTION

Post-secondary educational institutions can be viewed from a variety of different perspectives. For the majority of students and staff who work in them, they are centres of learning and teaching in which the participants are there by choice and consequently, by and large, work very hard. Research has always been important in some higher education institutions, but in recent years this emphasis has grown, and what for many was a great pleasure and, indeed, a treat, is becoming more of a threat and an insatiable performance indicator, which just has to be met. Maintaining the correct balance between quality research and learning/teaching, while the unit of resource continues to decline inexorably, is one of the key issues facing us all. Educational institutions as workplaces must be positive and not negative environments.

From another aspect, post-secondary educational institutions are clearly communities, functioning to all intents and purposes like small towns and internally requiring and providing a similar range of services, while also having very specialist needs. From yet another, they are seen as external suppliers of services to industry, commerce and the professions. These 'customers' receive, *inter alia*, a continuing flow of well qualified, fresh graduates with transferable skills; part-time and short course study opportunities through which to develop existing employees; consultancy services to solve problems and help expand business; and research and development support to create new breakthroughs.

However, educational institutions are also significant businesses in their own right. One recent study of the economic impact of higher education in Wales shows that it is of similar importance in employment terms to the steel or banking/finance sectors. Put another way, Welsh higher education institutions (HEIs) spend half a billion pounds annually and create more than 23,000 full-time equivalent jobs. And it must be remembered that there are only 13 HEIs in Wales, compared with more than 170 in the whole of the UK, and that these Welsh institutions are, on average, relatively small. In addition, it has recently been realized that UK higher education is a major export industry with the added benefit of long-term financial and political returns. If the UK further education sector is also added to this equation, then the economic impact of post-secondary education is of truly startling proportions.

Whatever perspective you take, it is obvious that educational institutions require managing and, consequently, this series has been produced to facilitate that end. The editors have striven to identify authors who are distinguished practitioners in their own right and, indeed, can also write. The authors have been given the challenge of producing essentially practical handbooks which combine appropriate theory and contextual material with many examples of good practice and guidance.

The topics chosen are of key importance to educational management and stand at the forefront of current debate. Some of these topics have never been covered in depth before and all of them are equally applicable to further as well as higher education. The editors are firmly of the belief that the UK distinction between these sectors will continue to blur and will be replaced, as in many other countries, by a continuum where the management issues are entirely common.

Since the mid-1980s, both of the editors have been involved with a management development programme for senior staff from HEIs throughout the world. Every year the participants quickly learn that we share the same problems and that similar solutions are normally applicable. Political and cultural differences may on occasion be important, but are often no more than an overlying veneer. Hence, this series will be of considerable relevance and value to post-secondary educational managers in many countries.

When the editors started their careers in higher education, the prevailing attitude towards the press (it was not known as 'the media' then) was totally defensive. If, and when, something went wrong in the institution, then it was the job of a senior member of staff to say as little as possible. He (almost invariably) was expected to play a straight bat and see off both the fast and spin bowling in the hope that some fortuitous circumstance (such as rain) would intervene and enable an honourable draw to be concluded. Of course, this English approach to crisis management or, at best, crisis mitigation, often failed miserably. And so, it gradually dawned on educational managers that a one-off reaction to events was inadequate and that there must be a continuous, proactive promotion of the institution to provide a positive context for future problems. This enlightenment was based on the truism that, 'doing a good job is only half the task; ensuring that the outside world knows that you are doing a good job is the way to complete victory'. In this way, the external relations function, encompassing all of the various areas of expertise described in this volume, was born.

External relations is now well developed in most post-secondary educational institutions, but we are still lagging behind many in 'the outside world' and, in particular, the United States. It is therefore especially pleasing that five of the team of experts whom Frank Albrighton and Julia Thomas have gathered together are not UK-based educationists. To emphasize further this interface between the educational and the outside world, we note that, by the time this book is published, Frank and Julia will have left the University of Birmingham to become joint principals of a communications and marketing consultancy. We have no doubt that they will be outstandingly successful.

David Warner
David Palfreyman

LIST OF FIGURES AND TABLES

Figures

1.1	The strategic approach to external relations	6
2.1	A selection of university logos	9
2.2	Brand strategy development	10
8.1	Responses to the question: 'Whose goodwill do you need?'	78
8.2	Responses to the question: 'Where do you get information about the university?'	81
8.3	Responses to the question: 'Where would you *prefer* to get information about the university?'	82

Tables

5.1	Activities involved in a product launch	45
11.1	Notional gift table for a £6 million target	113
11.2	Database subdivisions	115

PREFACE

When we were asked to edit this book, the publishers said it should be a 'how to' book. That is what we have tried to produce, but we do need to issue a small health warning. In recent years the whole business of external relations has become much more important in institutions of higher education. We are no longer self-conscious about discussing products, brands, market positions and all that. Policy-makers in institutions place external relations at the centre of strategic developments. It has ceased to be an optional add-on. Those engaged in external relations work are highly skilled professionals. They bring to the field an impressive array of expertise: in media relations, publications management, marketing, fundraising, alumni relations – all the topics discussed in the book. These people know their own minds and make a robust contribution to their organizations. They know a lot and have broad responsibilities.

We are fortunate that our own responsibilities at the University of Birmingham have included in one office the complete range of external relations activities, but we never considered writing the book and basing its precepts entirely on our own knowledge and experience. That would have been tedious for the reader and would have given only one perspective on what is a varied and changing scene. Far better that we should hear a variety of views from different institutions in the UK, United States and Australia. We are indebted to our colleagues who have contributed chapters to the book, sharing with us and with you the distillation of knowledge founded on high professional achievement. But those who do use the book as a practical manual should bear in mind that the circumstances of institutions vary in size, culture, organization and affluence. What may be appropriate in one may not work elsewhere.

Having said that, we do recommend studying and copying the success of others as a good strategy. We have learned a tremendous amount from fellow professionals in universities throughout the country and internationally, as well as from journalists, designers, market researchers and many others, and we want to acknowledge that.

We are also grateful to the members of the External Relations and Development Office at the University of Birmingham who are a highly professional team and have taught us much. In the preparation of this book, Hilary Gunton, Marilyn MacKenzie, Cheryl Needham and Katie Walker have been particularly helpful.

Frank Albrighton
Julia Thomas

NOTES ON CONTRIBUTORS

Peter Evans, broadcaster and journalist

Larry D. Lauer, Vice-Chancellor for Marketing and Communication, Texas Christian University, USA

Cyrrhian Macrae, Director, Corporate Affairs Unit, Coventry University

James Mahoney, Director, Public Affairs, The Australian National University

Reggie Simpson, Director of Alumni Relations, London School of Economics

Elizabeth Smith, Director of Development, University of Nottingham

Michael Stoner, Vice-President for New Media, Lipman Hearne, USA

Roger Stubbs, Deputy Managing Director, Market and Opinion Research International Ltd, London

WHAT IS EXTERNAL RELATIONS FOR?

Frank Albrighton and Julia Thomas

The great irony about public relations is that it has such a bad name. So much so that in the majority of higher education institutions the name is not even used and we settle more comfortably for 'external relations'. Years ago, the embryonic public relations offices had to be called 'information offices', implying that all they did was to transmit facts neutrally from the institution to the outside world. But external relations and public relations are the same thing and we must cope with the fact that the burgeoning public relations industry, dedicated to changing attitudes and improving opinions, has failed so signally to enhance its own reputation. Having a government that is repeatedly attacked for its reliance on spin and news management does not help.

The reasons why organizations undertake external relations activities apply just as much to higher education as elsewhere. All institutions need a good climate of opinion in which to flourish. It is not enough merely to be doing a good job, you must convince others that you are doing so. Beyond this, institutions, and especially those that rely predominantly on public funds, have a responsibility to external stakeholders to tell them what they are doing. This is not discharged satisfactorily through formal publications, annual reports and reports to funding councils. There is a duty to inform the general public in ways that are accessible, to tell them what they get for their money. At the same time, institutions have a duty to listen to what their stakeholders want and what they want them to do. External relations is a two-way process. In fact, it is more than two-way because although we use the phrase 'external relations', implying an interaction between those inside and those outside the institution, some of the most important constituencies that an institution should pay attention to are its own members: staff, students and alumni.

Although most people will agree quite readily that it is important to be accountable, to communicate with stakeholders and generally to relate to all our constituents, they are likely to pause a little when those worthy aspirations have a substantial price tag. External relations is not an end in itself and has no separate agenda from the institution. It must prove its value in competition with all the other demands on institutional funds.

The good news is that effective external relations will provide benefits for every area of an institution's work. It can help to recruit better students and staff. It can increase the generation of research income. It will improve the success rate of fundraising initiatives. There will be higher morale amongst staff who will become better motivated. The bad news is that these benefits are easy to assert but far more difficult to prove. It is curious that, for institutions that are dedicated to research and critical enquiry, in the matter of external relations the unsubstantiated assertion reigns supreme. We have all heard remarks from colleagues – not the most reliable sample – like, 'Of course, what people think of our institution is . . .' or, 'My son has read the prospectus and what he says is . . .' Not only are such assertions valueless, they can influence an institution's perceptions of itself and therefore its actions in damaging ways.

One institution established a research centre dedicated to a particular topic, confident that there was great demand for its services from industry and that it would easily secure external funding. This turned out not to be the case on either count. What had happened was that a senior academic, with a forceful personality, had asserted first that, 'people will come flocking to our door', and then that, 'the cost is no more than the chairman's tea money'. There are several lessons in this. First, do your market research on your product. Second, test the feasibility of your fundraising. And third – especially important if you are a professional communicator – note the persuasive effect of an argument expressed in vivid images.

Running through this book is the theme of measurement. There are ways to measure the effectiveness of external relations. Some of them, like systematic quantitative opinion research undertaken over a period of time, are authoritative and provide a statistical basis for evaluation. Others, what you might call second-level measures, can be derived from the success of the activities that external relations works to support: effective fundraising campaigns, the number of offers of help from alumni, an increase in applications from good potential students, and so on.

All these benefits are available to an institution that gets its external relations activities right. This book argues (effectively, we believe) that external relations is a highly professional activity that needs identified skills and a proper level of resources. But, more than that, the book offers practical guidance on how to obtain best value for money in a range of external relations activities and techniques, and then how to find out afterwards whether your money was well spent.

We have said that external relations is the same as public relations. Public relations has the reputation of being mere image-building. Is that all it is? No, but image is indeed part of what external relations is about. Some public relations practitioners take their business very seriously and work hard at complex definitions of what public relations is and what it means. One breathtakingly pretentious definition runs: 'a communication function of management through which organizations adapt to, alter, or maintain their environment for the purpose of achieving organizational goals.' What on earth does that mean? The mystification of external relations through obfuscation (as the author above might say) does nothing to help what is quite a straightforward process.

For a higher education institution we think it can be simply summed up as ensuring that the institution has the best reputation it deserves and that it benefits from that reputation. The 'deserves' is important. Even in higher education it is possible to spin a story, it is possible to extract the maximum from it, and it is even possible – dare we say it – to be economical with the truth. But it is not possible to build and sustain a reputation that is not founded on reality. Hype will be found out and will rebound on the institution. There was, many years ago, a British university that claimed that it had 'the loveliest campus in Europe'. Those who made the claim had clearly not crossed even their own county to look at other campuses, let alone visited the many beautiful universities around Europe. The claim was foolish and for anyone who stopped to think, that university became a laughing stock and its more serious claims of research and teaching quality were undermined.

At the other end of the scale, external relations, particularly the promotion of a good research reputation, can suffer from excessive academic reticence. Quite properly, academics are trained to be careful about what they claim for their work. Their reputations depend on it. But an institution's reputation depends on rather more robust statements than, 'I am only one of a team. The main work is being done over in America', or, 'I can't really claim that this is the most important development in this field because I haven't made a comprehensive study.'

At the University of Birmingham we recently undertook a review of our mission which included consultations with external stakeholders in the West Midlands. They were generally very proud of having what we claim is a world class university in their midst. But one of the things that they found irritating was our difficulty in identifying what we are best at. 'We accept your claim to be a world class university', they said, 'and we admire the fact that you carry out research and teach students in practically every discipline . . . But it defies common sense to claim that you are world class in absolutely every research area and in the teaching of absolutely every degree. Tell us what you are really good at.'

This is a hard question for a public relations officer and it is an even harder question for an institution. For decades, at least, the British university system has operated on the myth that all universities are as good as each other, all degrees are as good as each other and all departments are as good as each other. Increased selectivity, league tables of various kinds, research assessment exercises and all the rest have shown that this just is not true. We now coyly say that we are not *better* than each other we are just *different*. But no one is fooled. Potential students know which are the best universities for their subject. Employers know where they will get the best graduates for their kind of work, and newspapers happily refer to 'top' universities without receiving a murmur of complaint from anyone.

An effective external relations strategy has to be based on the reality of a reputation and on the reality of achievement, even if that means facing some uncomfortable facts about your institution's true worth. One of the greatest pitfalls for an institution is to develop an effective external relations machine, to devise powerful, positive messages, to communicate those messages widely and then to believe them. Yes, the messages must be based on reality and to that extent are believable, but they are an economical selection of the facts and so are vulnerable to questioning.

Perhaps it is because they often have a background as teachers, but some senior personnel in higher education can be prone to expounding what they think is good and important about their institution and expecting it to go unchallenged. The external relations professional has to be alert to this and reflect back to the institution how these claims will be received. This is where external relations is very much two-way. At the same time as you project the positive image, you must check it against reality and report back what you find. External relations reports the institution to the community and the community to the institution.

This reporting is not always welcomed. Individuals do not like to be told that their pet research project, far from being seen as ground-breaking, is capable of being mocked for its arcane preoccupations; that major new refurbishment that means so much to the head of department may be reduced by the journalist to: 'University opens new classroom'. The point is, do not believe your own propaganda; keep a sense of perspective and be brave enough to be the messenger with the bad news. Sometimes this will be trivial – like the examples above – but sometimes it will be serious.

External relations must also be based on some kind of system. It is not about being nice to people. It is not about drinking gin and tonic or receiving courteous thank-you letters after sumptuous dinners in the vice-chancellor's residence. It is about identifying those groups whose actions can affect the welfare of an institution and prioritizing your work accordingly. Some key groups are obvious. You need potential students to think well enough of your institution to apply for your courses. You need research funders to rate highly your academic staff. Beyond that you need the local authority to have enough respect for the institution to be sympathetic to planning applications. You need governments internationally to recognize the strength of your qualifications. The list of constituencies can be very long: teachers, parents, local residents, civil servants, alumni, media, employers, the professions, the academic community, potential staff, present staff, benefactors, potential benefactors, and so on. Many of these will overlap. Consider the individual who, over a number of years, may be a potential student, student, alumnus, parent of student, local resident, local councillor, industrial partner, and benefactor.

There is a lesson here too. Just as you cannot be all things to all people, so you cannot be different things to different people. The institution must have a clear perception of itself that is presented consistently to all audiences. The present emphasis on widening participation raises some interesting questions. How does an institution that prides itself on research of international quality and attracts students with the highest qualifications present itself to those with no knowledge of higher education and who offer experience and qualifications that differ greatly from those of 18-year-olds just leaving school? Is it possible to maintain quality whilst making radical changes of culture? It is, but it will create some formidable challenges for those who have to ensure that public opinion keeps pace with those changes.

It is important not to become daunted by the magnitude of the many audiences and the complex messages. Part of the strategic approach to external relations involves identifying those audiences that are most important to you and having a clear idea of what you

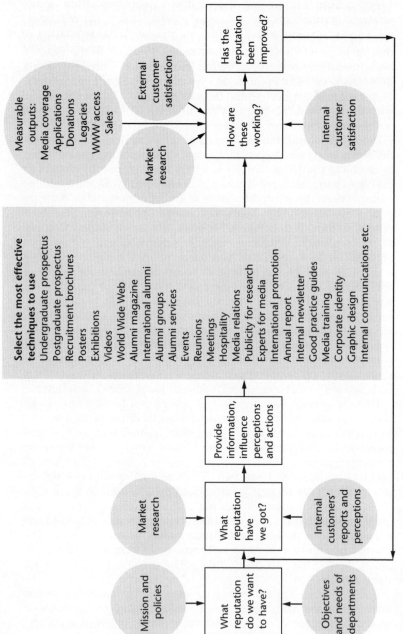

Figure 1.1 The strategic approach to external relations

want them to think of you and what you want them to do. So the strategic thinking should run something like this: What reputation do we want to have with this group of people? What reputation *do* we have with them? How wide is the discrepancy? On what do people base their judgement? Where do they get their information from?

The answers to these questions tell you what additional information you must provide and by what means. When you have given your target group the further information through the most effective techniques you can go back and find out whether your reputation has actually improved. Figure 1.1 shows the process in diagrammatic form.

Only by approaching external relations in a managed, measured way can you hope to achieve anything worthwhile. Too often something is presented with, 'this will be good public relations', when the proponent has no idea what effect it will have or on whom. It is an excuse for trying something merely because it is novel or, in the world of devolved departmental budgets, as a technique for persuading the external relations office to pay for it. Good external relations work knows what it is doing, why it is doing it and whether it worked.

2

A ROSE BY ANY OTHER NAME
Brand management and
visual identity

Frank Albrighton and
Julia Thomas

Juliet got it wrong. Names do matter – as she found out to her cost and for which she paid the ultimate price.

Names are important because they communicate the essential identity of the person, the thing or the activity for which they provide a badge. In the world of consumer products, everything has a name, a name that is designed to entice, beguile and persuade. Everything has a logo. A logo that is designed to catch the attention and suggest positive values of a product or service. The spread of visual identities has been phenomenal in recent years. Nowhere nowadays do you see a shopfront with a simple unadorned name of the proprietor – unless, of course, that person *is* the brand. One-person businesses have their symbols and slogans. Major companies promote their identities everywhere, even when they have nothing to say other than 'we are here'. An accurate description, however comprehensive, is not enough.

It is not so long ago that a few forward-looking institutions of higher education in the UK were derided for adopting the conventions of the marketplace and commissioning logos and corporate identities. They were accused of being brash and insecure, needing to adopt the promotional techniques of the marketplace when surely a sound reputation would be sufficient. Now, turning the pages of the *Times Higher Education Supplement* shows that, almost without exception,

THE UNIVERSITY
OF BIRMINGHAM

LONDON GUILDHALL
UNIVERSITY

COVENTRY
UNIVERSITY

Figure 2.1 A selection of university logos

institutions have carefully researched and professionally designed
logos and positioning statements to attach to their job advertisements.
These styles are carried through rigorously in publications, websites
and other materials. Figure 2.1 shows a selection of these logos.

A name and a visual identity are not ends in themselves: they must

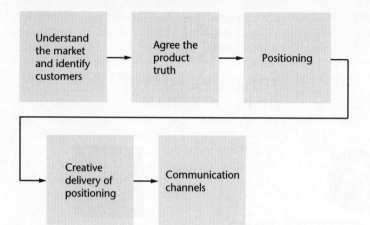

Figure 2.2 Brand strategy development

be the expression of the true identity of the institution. They are not just a graphic device that looks good: they should be a visual expression of what the institution stands for. The whole of an institution's visual identity should be the product of its brand positioning and not the beginning of it.

Speaking at a seminar of public relations officers from members of the international group Universitas 21,[1] Marie Oldham, Business Development Director of BBC Worldwide, talked about the principles of brand management and discussed whether or not they were applicable to universities. She described five key stages in what is known as brand strategy development. This is expressed in Figure 2.2. Some of these stages are related easily to higher education. 'Understand the market and identify customers' makes us think immediately of student recruitment. At the other end of the process, communication channels are familiar: publications, World Wide Web, the media, alumni relations and so on. But what about those stages in between, to what extent are they applicable in higher education?

'Agree the product truth'. Before we shy away from the marketing language, what might that mean for higher education institutions? In commerce, it describes the process of trying to reduce the essential values and qualities of the product to a brief statement, often to a single word. This is very difficult for us. Mission statements are either too long and self-indulgent or utterly banal. We claim distinctiveness for our institutions but find it difficult to identify the qualities that make us distinctive.

At a regular national training course for new entrants to the profession of educational administration, it has been our practice during a session on external relations to invite each member of the group to devise a sentence that describes uniquely their own institution. Naturally the participants aré reluctant to offer bad qualities as their unique selling points: 'The only institution never to have had a grade 5 research rating or an excellent teaching quality assessment'. They then spend some time mulling over the positive attributes, but find that everyone in the group is claiming excellence, quality, flexibility and all the rest. In the end we find that, for the majority of institutions, the only truly distinctive quality is their address.

Even if you can agree on your product truth, positioning, the third key stage, is very difficult. It is hard to differentiate, except in marginal areas, between institutions of higher education that belong to the broad groupings with which we are familiar.

Without a clear sense of what our positioning is, its creative delivery, stage four, becomes very difficult and we often find that communication channels and techniques are used which merely recycle the familiar and undistinctive. There are catchphrases that we use in a variety of different combinations. For the budding author of mission statements and strategic plans, here is a ready-made vocabulary suitable for all purposes:

excellence	attractive setting
high quality	good communications
research-led	responsive
demand-led	new teaching methods
international	friendly staff
good facilities	lifelong learning
forward-looking	post-Dearing agenda
new millennium	management of change
leadership	local community
partnership	new technology
collaboration with industry	flexible

In her presentation to the Universitas 21 members, Marie Oldham went on to discuss some of the usual arguments *against* the adoption of a carefully managed brand strategy.

'We have diverse target audiences'

Yes we do, but so does an airline, for example. In addition to the traveller, these can be divided between those who make decisions and those who influence decisions. The decision-makers include travel agents, corporate travel managers and the traveller's secretary or assistant who may make bookings. Those who influence travel decisions include government and the media. Airlines are rigorous at adopting a clear visual identity that literally flies around the world on their products and then reduce their core propositions to a single phrase. Ideas like: 'Fly the flag', 'The world's favourite airline', '21st century air travel'.

The way that an airline relates to its different markets is not to change the visual presentation or compromise the core message but to use one style to offer different products and different benefits through different communications channels. This is the way to ensure that you say the right thing to the right people in an appropriate tone of voice and in an accessible context, without confusing your audience about what it is that you stand for.

'We have more than one corporate position'

Do you really? Think about the brand Virgin. Over the years this brand has been applied to an extraordinarily wide range of products, targeting a very wide range of audiences. There has always been an underlying core proposition in the person of Sir Richard Branson, who is consistently voted the most popular business leader. Virgin stands for breaking the rules for the benefit of the customer.

When the brand was applied to pensions and banking, the message was that Virgin was challenging the big boys, providing a service that was honest and accountable. The Virgin airline again challenged the big boys. It was flexible, entertaining and provided true value for money. The record shops had fair prices, convenient opening hours and a welcoming and relaxed atmosphere. Similar attributes applied to Virgin cola and other Virgin products and services.

The Virgin brand has achieved a quite remarkable level of recognition and positive association by adopting a simple core proposition and sticking to it.

'We need a different market position when we are operating in different markets'

Marie Oldham's engaging way of dealing with this objection was to speculate on the nature of products that leading brand names might offer if they moved into an entirely different market. If Volvo produced a mobile phone, what would be the main message? It would be safe. If there were a Häagen-Dazs range of food, what would it be like? Luxury, premium priced and full-fat. If the BBC designed an internet site, what would it feel like? It would be for everyone, British, demonstrate high skills, be unbiased and offer a mixture of entertainment, information and education.

How is it that we can make these extrapolations so readily? It is because we recognize and understand the core values of the brand names and we assume that those values apply to any product. It is important to build on core values and allow the customer's experience of the brand in other contexts to deliver understanding, awareness and approval in the new market.

'Customers don't know what they need'

This is the most plausible counter-argument in a higher education context. How can students know what they should be taught? How can researchers know where their enquiries will lead? They cannot, of course; but the political reality is that students are powerful customers and their wishes have to be taken into account. Research is not only curiosity-driven: it is funded by external partners who want results of one kind or another. Higher education institutions have to reconcile these conflicting influences, being careful not to allow either to dominate.

All this marketing-speak may seem remote from your daily life in an institution of higher education. Is it the rarified theorizing of the world of commerce unrelated to practical matters in higher education? What does it mean in practice to have a clear identity, and what are the dangers of not having one? One of the acknowledged gurus of corporate identity is Wally Olins.[2] He said:

> Identity: What is it?
>
> In order to be effective every organisation needs a clear sense of purpose that people within it understand. They also need a strong sense of belonging.
>
> Purpose and belonging are the two facets of identity.
>
> Every organisation is unique, and the identity must spring from the organisation's own roots, its personality, its strengths and its weaknesses.
>
> This is as true of the modern global corporation as it has been of any other institution in history, from the Christian church to the nation state.
>
> The identity of the corporation must be so clear that it becomes the yardstick against which its products, behaviour and actions are measured.

This means that the identity cannot simply be a slogan, a collection of phrases: it must be visible, tangible and all-embracing.

Everything that the organisation does must be an affirmation of its identity.

The *products* that the company makes or sells must project its standards and its values.

The *buildings* in which it makes things and trades, its offices, factories and showpieces – their location, how they are furnished and maintained – are all manifestations of identity.

The corporation's *communication material,* from its advertising to its instruction manuals, must have a consistent quality and character that accurately and honestly reflect the whole organisation and its aims.

All these are palpable, they are visible; they are designed – and that is why design is a significant component in the identity mix.

A further component, which is just as significant although it is not visible, is how the organisation behaves: to its own staff and to everybody with whom it comes into contact, including customers, suppliers and its host communities. This is especially true in service industries that have no tangible products. Here, too, consistency in attitude, action and style underlines the corporation's identity.

In small companies and in young companies the management of identity is intuitive. It is a direct reflection of the founder's obsessions and interests. The company is what he or she makes it.

In the sprawling, complex corporations with which this book is mostly concerned, where innumerable interests – each supported by individuals – conflict and compete for power and influence, the company's long-term purpose, its values, its identity must be managed consciously and clearly, or they will be overwhelmed and disregarded in sectional infighting. The organisation will simply become an inert victim of the various factions that seek to control it.

Hands up anyone who recognizes 'an inert victim of the various factions that seek to control it'. The stakes are high and you need advances on a number of fronts – many of them described in this book – to protect an institution from the ravages that Olins describes.

The big issues have to be resolved by the institution through consensus and at the highest level: what is our mission, how shall we achieve it, what are our long-term strategies? There will come a stage, however, when the agreed principles, the core proposition, the mission, however you choose to describe them, have to be expressed in the visual identity. This is no mere mechanical exercise. All the tensions within an institution will emerge as a new identity is devised and implemented. If there are internal struggles then the visual identity provides an apparently safe and inconsequential battleground upon which they can be fought out. The corporate identity police become the target for all the resentment, jealousy and frustrations that members in units of the institution feel towards its management. A visual identity is an expression of corporate authority and as such may be resisted by some.

Nevertheless, many institutions successfully introduce and maintain visual identities that serve the purposes of the institution well. How do they go about it? First of all, it is important to take stock of the present situation. For its first 135 years, the University of Massachusetts at Amherst never had an official logo. By the mid-1990s its many schools, departments, programmes and other units had created 137 unofficial ones – more than one for every year of the institution's existence. This is the situation that will be recognizable to many in British institutions of higher education.

Faced with this situation, or with the need to replace a visual identity that has outlived its appropriateness, the process of introducing a new visual identity can be planned in four key stages.

1 What do we want to say?

It is very easy to leap ahead to thinking about logos and typefaces as if they were ends in themselves. A successful visual identity will be grounded in thorough research about the nature of the institution and about its aspirations. This may be conducted by the institution itself, but ideally should involve outside consultants in order to achieve the necessary degree of objectivity. An inspirational speech by the head of the institution does not equal everything that must be said about it. The visual identity should be something that can be owned by all members of the institution. The members should be able to relate to it as an expression of the organization for which they work and the aims towards which they are progressing. Opinion research inside and outside the institution will discover how it wishes to be perceived and how it is actually perceived. The visual identity can help to move matters forward. Although a new visual identity is about change, it should not become change for change's sake. If there are powerful positive aspects to an institution's reputation – it is reliable and respectable, for example – these should not be thrown out in an attempt to achieve some kind of modern raciness that is entirely inappropriate.

This stage of devising the visual identity is exactly the same as that of devising the brand identity. They are the same thing. What kind of institution do we have? What are the values for which it stands? What is our core proposition? The answers to these questions will provide the essential ingredients of the brief to the design consultant who must turn these ideas into something visual.

2   Look and feel

The design consultants will take away these concepts and return with a visual expression of them. When the designers return, what they show you could take many forms. It might be just a way of writing your name. It might be a stylized picture of one of your principal buildings. It might be based upon the institution's crest. It might be an image or symbol that you had never thought of.

It may delight, it may surprise, it may even shock. For you, it may be love at first sight. You may feel cold indifference or you may take an instant dislike to what you are being shown. In one sense, that does not matter at all. What is important is whether the graphic designs communicate accurately and effectively the corporate messages that you have adopted. As someone who understands those messages as thoroughly as anyone, and especially if you have been involved in communicating them in the briefing to the designer, you can reasonably expect the design to work for you. But be careful to suppress personal preferences that may cloud your judgement about the communicative efficiency of what you are looking at.

If you have planned and managed the process to this stage you can probably achieve this objectivity. It will be much more difficult to control the reactions of others. It is probably unavoidable that the first time the design proposals are shown to groups within the institution, reactions will quickly degenerate into, 'I like this', 'I don't like that'. It is, however, important that members of the institution should be given a choice and not presented with a *fait accompli*. The adoption of the visual identity must, as far as possible, be a shared project and not one imposed by the professionals. Probably the best way forward is for the external relations department and the design consultants to agree a range of proposals, all of which meet the communications requirements but with different emphases on different aspects. This range of proposals can then be shown to the chief executive and any appropriate body for a final decision.

3   Making it work in practice

The initial design proposals are likely to have consisted of not much more than the logo, the styling of the name of the institution, and one or two important areas like stationery. The professionalism of the graphic designers should have taken into account that there will be a wide range of applications that have to be accommodated over many years. Even so, there must now be a stage of careful development of the ideas, working out exactly how they will be put into practice in this wide range of contexts. The list of applications will be quite long and will include some or all of the following.

* stationery: letterheads, memos, compliment slips, business cards, envelopes
* forms: invoices, purchase orders, application forms
* publications: prospectuses, annual reports, brochures, leaflets, maps
* vehicles
* advertising
* gifts and souvenirs
* signs
* exhibitions
* clothing.

In some contexts it will be appropriate to extend the visual identity into interior design of reception areas, visitor centres and so on.

In each of these categories there will massive detail that has to be worked through. The problems have to be resolved at some stage and it is better if they can be sorted out before implementation rather than afterwards. The matters that have to be resolved will not only be visual; there will also be, for example, documents that have legal implications where the institution does not have complete control over what is included or how it is presented. In most institutions of higher education there is a great variety of computer hardware and software: care must be taken to ensure that any new templates or standards are widely accessible.

The process of discussion and consultation with individual units throughout the institution will help to raise awareness of the impending change and increase the sense of ownership. The outcome of all these discussions and intensive work by the design consultants will be a visual identity manual. Nowadays, this should be produced not only in paper form but also electronically, probably on CD and downloadable from the institution's intranet. A word of caution about the web, however: documents downloaded can very often be altered by the recipient and you must be careful about the enthusiast who thinks the logo is pretty good but would be enhanced if only it were presented in 3D format and made to revolve.

4   Making it happen

At one end of the scale, the introduction of a new visual identity can constitute a major relaunch for the organization itself. Commercial companies will have new names, new shopfronts, new vehicles, new publications, new stationery, new everything on a given date. Massive changes are made overnight. Higher education institutions are unlikely to have either the inclination or the resources to do that.

Nevertheless, it is important to think about whether there is to be a launch date. Almost certainly it will not be possible to arrange matters so that the new visual identity starts on a particular day and all manifestations of previous versions disappear. It is important, however, that there should be a stage beyond which old material will not be used. There may be individuals who are so fond of the past that they will try to carry on using their favourite letterhead, perhaps even designed by themselves, for as long as possible. If this happens, it is evidence that the individual has not understood why the new visual identity is important and how it can help their work. It is unlikely that everyone in the institution will have been so interested or involved in the process of planning for the new visual identity that they will be fully committed to its value and work hard on its implementation. The implementation process has a continuing educational role, introducing the principles behind the visual identity and persuading everyone that the new scheme does not threaten their autonomy or impinge on academic freedom but will indeed help them better to fulfil their own ambitions. This is the carrot, but there does have to be an element of stick.

Discussions about the visual identity cannot go on for ever and there comes a point when the institution must have its way. It should be possible to avoid, in all but the most extreme cases, a direct confrontation between the policy of the visual identity and individual units. It is, however, important that those charged with implementation should have the clear authority of the institution and the chief executive. The policy can very easily be undermined.

Imagine a situation in which the leader of a powerful research group, attracting millions of pounds in support, feels strongly that their unit's publicity material should be distinctive and different from that of the parent institution. This can be presented to the chief executive as a minor matter to do with logos and letterheaded paper, but one which can become an irritation if the head of the research group does not have their way. The way to deal with this is for it to be made clear from the outset that the external relations department, charged with implementing the new policy, has the confidence and authority of the chief executive. No one else should be drawn into negotiations, making concessions or offering deals. If they are, the corporate identity implementation team will quickly lose heart and back away from any difficult issues. The visual identity will be compromised, and so, progressively, will the whole brand identity of the institution.

We are back where we started. We must have firm institutional commitment to a clear brand identity expressed through corporate positioning and visual identity.

Notes

1 M. Oldham (1999) Integrated marketing. Unpublished proceedings of Universitas 21 Professional Seminar on Communications, Alumni Relations and Development, University of Birmingham.
2 W. Olins (1989) *Corporate Identity*. London: Thames and Hudson, p.7.

3

SO THAT'S WHAT THEY THINK
Market research

Roger Stubbs

Higher education is a competitive market. There are plenty of 'customers' – three times the proportion of 18-year-olds now go on to higher education than was the case in 1980. But therein lies the problem: how do you maintain the standards of entry?

It is important to maintain entry standards if the value of your qualifications is not to diminish, which would make it harder to attract top academics and, in turn, funds for research and government support. Employers would set less store by your degrees, and this in turn discourages top students from applying – a particularly dangerous downward spiral.

So, like any other marketplace, the suppliers that produce the best (or more popular) products and/or promote them most effectively are likely to be the most successful. To achieve this position, a keen understanding is required of the customer's requirements, and the processes used to reach a 'purchase' decision. This is one of the prime roles which market research can play.

The role of opinion research

Why is it that relatively few higher education establishments undertake market research? I suspect in many cases the answer is that they believe they do. They interview lots of applicants and get feedback from their colleagues in individual departments on what students said, the questions they asked, how they reacted to the premises, the course content, the staff. This gives a sense of being close to student opinion. But this is anecdotal and illusory. Students, indeed any group of people, are highly selective on the feedback they provide to a potential employer or any organization to which they are in some sense applying.

The only way to obtain impartial, reliable and accurate information on people's opinions and values is to conduct an opinion survey which is properly constructed and professionally carried out. Like any other service, the potential benefits need to be weighed against the cost of achieving them. There would be no point in spending £5000 on a survey which is likely to generate benefits of a few hundred pounds at most. The problem is that the potential benefits are sometimes difficult to estimate, so judgement has to be used in most situations. In reality, however, clients can usually identify quite easily those areas on which research expenditure is justified.

As this chapter unfolds, we will try to combine a primer in market research principles and practice with examples to illustrate actual and potential applications in the higher education field.

Examples of higher education research

The following examples have been undertaken on behalf of a variety of institutions:

- Determining how universities are selected for undergraduate and postgraduate courses among domestic and overseas audiences and their advisers. Similar work conducted for specific departments.
- Exploring why students decided to select another institution.
- Helping to design and refine prospectuses, videos and websites and reaction to a CD-ROM version of the prospectus.
- Assessing the demand for postgraduate courses to be offered on a part-time basis.
- Establishing your competitive position against other institutions and the 'ideal' place to study.
- Estimating the level and scope of interest in higher education courses among the wider general public, especially those from disadvantaged areas.
- Measuring satisfaction with and projected demand for student accommodation of various types.
- Understanding the image of different universities among a variety of audiences including the general public, teachers, employees, sixth-formers and alumni.

- Learning how much value is attached by the local community to having a medical school in the locality, for residents, local government officials and general practitioners.
- Providing input for a new mission statement.
- Reviewing prices of accommodation at different universities.
- Reviewing speed of responding to enquiries from students.
- Quantifying the demand for facilities for conference centres during vacation weeks.
- Evaluating attitudes of alumni to a new specialist publication or to proposed activities or events.
- Finding out how opinion leaders, for example education journalists, personnel directors and MPs, view the institution and how best to communicate with these groups.

Decisions made by universities concerning external relations are likely to be better if they are made in the knowledge of the views of relevant audiences rather than without it. But in addition to using research to improve and inform management decision-making, it can also have a public relations value. Rarely a day goes by without the findings of some survey or other being featured in the media. Many of these are commissioned by organizations wishing to make a point ('advocacy polls') or to establish themselves as the recognized authority on a particular issue. As yet, the higher education sector has made little use of surveys for this purpose, but as competition intensifies, such usage may well proliferate.

One of the first such uses was by the University of Birmingham, to test the effect on its national reputation of the BBC's using its campus to film a dramatization of David Lodge's book, *Nice Work*. There was some concern that the association of such 'entertainment' with the campus might damage the university. In the event, the picturesque campus shots significantly enhanced awareness and the image of the university.

How does market research work?

Market research exists to gather information about people or topics, usually so that an organization can make better-informed decisions. The three key aspects of this are *how* to gather the information, *from whom*, and *from how many* respondents. In covering these issues we shall encounter and explain a few technical terms. Many are words we use in our everyday lives, but which have a distinct and specific meaning in the world of market research – error, random, significant, universe, sample.

How to gather the information ▮

One technique that might be used to gather information is to see what is already available (secondary research). A large number of bodies publish statistical data, from government departments and universities to trade bodies and individual corporations. A great deal of 'opinion' survey data is also readily available: at any one time the MORI website shows detailed findings from dozens of recent surveys, all in the public domain.

It is a good idea to check that someone else has not already conducted the survey you want to do, or something very similar, before you spend considerable sums of money doing it yourself. This searching for existing information is called 'desk research', and should never be overlooked. Mostly, though, market research is concerned with primary data collection, and the following outlines the many ways of going about it.

Self-completion

On the face of it, a postal survey is very attractive: you mail questionnaires to potential respondents who complete them at a time convenient to themselves and send the completed forms back in a reply-paid envelope. Straightforward, inexpensive. But usually worthless. Unless the topic is of particular interest to the respondent (e.g. we surveyed head teachers this way on the issue of teaching law in schools on behalf of the Law Society and achieved a 76 per cent response rate), the response rate is likely to be low – sometimes below 10 per cent. The low numbers themselves are not a problem – you just do a larger mail-out – but the likelihood is strong that those who do reply are atypical; they feel particularly strongly about the subject, or have an axe to grind. And research which is unrepresentative is likely to be worse than no research at all. There is also no control over who actually completes the questionnaire – your intended senior manager may delegate the job to a member of staff, for example. These problems are magnified when using the internet to conduct surveys, a development which is already having a major influence on the opinion research business. Self-completion does work very well though where the audience is the workforce, or for some situations in higher education, the student population.

Telephone

The telephone survey is an excellent way of polling people who use the telephone extensively in their day-to-day lives, such as businesspeople, or school-leavers before they embark on higher education. A further advantage of the telephone survey is the wide geographical spread which can be achieved. Quicker and cheaper than face-to-face interviews, which are usually 'clustered' to keep costs within bounds, the two main drawbacks of telephone surveys are the inability to use visual stimuli (lists on cards, logos, advertisements) and time constraint of 15–20 minutes. However, an experienced researcher can design questions to elicit a lot of information in 15 minutes.

Face-to-face

The restrictions of telephone surveys do not apply to personal interviews, and there is an added benefit of a rapport established between interviewer and respondent which can enhance the quality of responses, particularly to open-ended questions. Personal interviews are, however, the most expensive of the three options where executive audiences are involved. For the general public, though, face-to-face interviews are cost-effective. Contrary to the popular image, most are *not* conducted in the street. MORI undertakes almost all its general public interviewing in respondents' homes.

Sometimes, personal interviewing can actually cost less per interview than telephone interviewing. For example, in a survey designed to explore the possibilities of wider access to higher education courses, we wanted to focus attention on the more depressed localities of a region. This is difficult to do by telephone because exchanges can cover wide areas, and in research terms, difficult translates into expensive.

Many clients require highly reliable information on a limited range of issues. *Omnibus surveys* were designed for this purpose. These consist of a large – usually 1000 or 2000 – representative sample of the adult general public on which several clients place questions. No client sees any other client's questions or results, and the costs are spread across all the sponsors. These are usually priced on a per-question basis and provide a highly cost-effective way of obtaining reliable data – frequently a few thousand pounds for very detailed data.

Qualitative research

Up to this point we have focused on quantitative research, the traditional image of surveys – a structured questionnaire administered in some way to a substantial sample population. Yet there are occasions when a less formal approach is preferable. For example, when trying to understand how sixth-formers decide which universities to put on their UCAS forms, or how they use prospectuses, or their reactions to a proposed video or website, the interest is not on measurement but on insight and understanding: what do they do, think or believe, and why. 'Why' is the most useful word in qualitative research. For such a purpose, a small number of fairly unstructured in-depth interviews, or one or two group discussions may be adequate. These techniques go under the general heading of 'qualitative research'.

One-to-one interviews are useful when there is a need to explore the detailed experience of one individual, such as the process used by a major industrial company to allocate research funds to universities. Very often, though, the 'added value' of qualitative work lies in the interaction among respondents. Think, for example, of listening to a sixth-form student describing how he/she would select universities. The basic theme may well be a mix of the course wanted and expected A-level results. Then another participant interrupts:

'No – I'd want to go to a big city.'
'Why's that?'
'The night-life, shops and eating places.'

Another points out that:

'It's got to be somewhere close, so I can live at home. I can't afford to move away.'

Which causes someone else to chime in:

'I'd never want to do that – I want freedom from Mum and Dad's control.'

All of these issues can be explored and the pros and cons discussed; finally, the reasons can be analysed by a skilled group moderator.

These sessions can be great fun, and highly informative, to sit in on: no matter how well a report on the event is written, it is not the same as being there. Hearing your real customers discussing your product offering and the purchase motivations can be an eye-opening experience. Even hearing the terminology they use, rather than the terms you use, can be enormously helpful in designing literature. Unless the subject matter is sensitive, most research agencies will be delighted to have a client representative or two sitting in. Do so whenever you can: it is rare to get such first-hand impressions, and you may even pick up some of the moderator's skills. Almost without exception, the participants enjoy the experience: it is not every day that someone wants to hear their opinion, let alone is willing to pay for it (it is usual to make a token payment of around £20 as a thank-you for attending, and to cover expenses).

How to choose

With such a proliferation of techniques to choose from, how do you choose 'the best'? This is where you need the guidance of an experienced research practitioner. He or she will be able to offer informed advice. However, in order to do that, you will need to be as clear as you can about the objectives of the research and the way in which the findings may be used. For example, if you want to set a benchmark for the image of your institution, or how well informed staff and students feel, against which you can measure progress in the future, you need numerical data with substantial samples; qualitative work alone will not suffice. Equally, if you want to understand the subtleties of the way that various audiences feel about your mission statement, or the messages that people take from a proposed advertisement, structured questions with large samples just will not achieve that: you need the abilities of a qualitative researcher to tease out the insights involved.

One qualitative project designed to evaluate prospectuses provided a nice example of 'disaster-check', generally used in advertising research. The prospectus was highly regarded in terms of content, layout and format, but one phrase in it – intended to imply that its students are high achievers – succeeded in raising the hackles of virtually all the sixth-formers. They described it as elitist. The research paid for itself with that finding alone.

So, use *qualitative* research when:

- exploring a new issue on which you have little idea of how the intended audience will react
- you want to understand the basic way a process works, or the key criteria on which something is assessed and the terminology used by people to describe it
- you need help in interpreting data from a quantitative study: Why do overseas students rate the selection process so poorly? Why are open days at Bristol rated better than those at Manchester? Why is your institution not viewed as forward-looking?

You can see that qualitative work may be undertaken in conjunction with quantitative – usually in advance of, but sometimes as a follow-up stage.

Use *quantitative* research when:

- you are pretty sure that you know what the issues are but you need to prioritize them
- you are trying to assess the potential demand for something – a new type of post-graduate course, self-contained accommodation, using facilities for conferences
- you need to measure opinions, beliefs or behaviour, especially if you need to understand how various audiences differ – undergraduates and postgraduates, students living at home vs away from home, local residents vs national public opinion, older vs younger people, those who accepted vs rejected your offer.

Even if it is clear which type of research – qualitative or quantitative – your project requires, we have seen that there are many different techniques within each family. Involve your research supplier in the decision about the specific technique which will be best in the circumstances. Indeed, ask two or three research agencies to come up with proposals. Market research is a competitive business, and agencies will not mind being invited to tender. Often there is no best approach, and it is useful to hear the pros and cons of the options discussed by various agencies.

Whom to survey? The principles of sampling

Market researchers can be irritatingly practical. You have a pretty good idea of what you want to research – let's say it is how sixth-form students decide which universities to apply to. That is clear enough, surely? Not for the researcher; he/she will want to know the scope of your audience. *Do you mean students from state schools, independent schools or sixth-form colleges?* Easy, all three. *OK, any students taking A-levels?* Well, any expecting to achieve at least a specified standard. *Include Scotland?* Er, we traditionally don't get many applications from there. *Overseas-based students?* Well, they are an important revenue-earner. *Including them will add significantly to the budget.* Ah, well, perhaps we'll leave them out this time; that's all agreed then. *While you're at it, shouldn't you be finding out what students think of your institution?* Good idea, we can do that in the same study, can't we? *Up to a point, but wouldn't it be useful to talk to a few first-years here and discover why they decided to come?* Yes, we should do that. *But what of those who applied here but went elsewhere, or those who didn't even apply?*

You see the point. Frequently, these early discussions act as a catalyst to refine or develop the research objectives. A good researcher will look for ways to add value to the study and to help you think through what you really need the data for, how the data are likely to be used and the most cost-effective research design.

Having agreed your audience(s), the next issues are how to select a sample and how many to sample.

Sampling

We define a sample as 'a selection of entries drawn from a population in such a way that the sample represents the population being surveyed'. By 'population', a researcher does not necessarily mean the general public. A population (or universe) refers to all the people in a particular definable group. It might be all alumni, all secondary school teachers with a careers advisory function, all academic staff at a particular institution, or, going back to the above example, all first-year A-level students in England and Wales who expect to achieve at least a specified standard.

In a researcher's world, 'sample' is not just a 'few members' of a population, but a number selected in such a way that they have the same characteristics as the population from which they are drawn: they are 'representative' of that population. A random sample is one in which every member of the population has the same, non-zero, chance of being selected. In some cases, achieving a random sample is easy: an institution will have a list of all its academic staff, so if you want a sample of 60 from 300, you could choose every fifth name (choosing a starting point from 1 to 5 at random).

Often, though, it is not at all straightforward. Take alumni, for example. The institution loses touch with many alumni over the years, perhaps retaining contact with higher proportions of those who graduated more recently. So any list of alumni has major omissions. In such a case the only practical option is to use that list, but any sample drawn from it is unlikely to be representative of all alumni. It would be weighted towards younger members and those who, by definition, are interested enough in their alma mater to keep it informed of their whereabouts.

Even in situations where it is possible to draw a 'representative' sample, not all those selected will be willing to take part, and there is always a worry about what the survey findings would have looked like if all *had* taken part. Market research is a simple business conceptually – ask the right people the right questions and add up the numbers correctly – but the practical realities in trying to achieve this often render it highly complex. Which is another reason why you need expert help.

How large a sample?

One question which researchers are frequently asked by their client is the very reasonable: 'how many do we need in the sample for the results to be reliable?' It is one of the toughest to answer; books have been written about it. All I will attempt to do here is to set out some of the basic facts of sampling life:

- The conventional way in which the reliability of a statistic from a sample is measured is the '95 per cent confidence interval'. Let us say we have a sample of 200, which generates a finding that 30 per cent hold a particular view. We can be 95 per cent sure that the 'true' figure, i.e. the one we would have found if every member of the population had been surveyed, would be within 6 per cent either way of this, i.e. that between 24 per cent and 36 per cent of the total population hold the particular view. Another way of thinking of this is that in 19 cases out of 20, a sample of 200 will give a value within 6 percentage points of the true one.

  It is unfortunate that these tolerances differ for different percentage results. In other words, using the example above, if 50 per cent held a particular view, the 95 per cent confidence interval would be plus or minus *seven* percentage points. For the mathematically minded, these intervals are calculated as follows:

  $$95\% \text{ confidence interval} = 1.96\sqrt{\frac{P(1-P)}{n}}$$

  where P is percentage result (expressed as a decimal) and n is sample size, and the square-root expression is known as the 'standard error'.
- 'Significant differences' are those which statistically have less than 5 per cent probability of occurring by chance. They may or may not be deemed important – that is a value judgement.
- Bigger samples are better. No surprise there, but the reliability does not improve in proportion to the sample size. The square root sign in the formula means that, to be twice as good, you need four times as many in the sample, and to be three times as good, nine times as many.

  Also, if the sample is not representative of the universe, then bigger is not better – it just extends the bias. Many years ago a right-wing newspaper claimed wondrous accuracy for a coupon-return political survey of its readers – nearly 100,000. It may have been accurate as a survey of its readers, but the contemporary MORI opinion poll, sample size 2000, gave a much better indication of the views of the British general public.

- Larger samples cost more money. The real trick in research surveys is balancing utility against cost. If you are brand manager for a breakfast cereal, and your job is on the line if your market share falls more than 0.2 per cent, then it may well be worth going for a huge sample. But if you want to gauge whether your new logo is seen as superior to the old, you are unlikely to be concerned if the score is 80:20 or 70:30, so a small sample will suffice. Again, seek guidance from an expert.
- It is often not the reliability of the *total* sample which is critical, but how many *subgroups* you might want to examine. In a survey of the general public you may be particularly interested in how responses differ by age group. In this case, the number in each age group cell would govern the calculations of reliability, and therefore sample size required.
- Size of population has little effect on these calculations. Whether your 200 is from a universe of 4000 or 40 million makes almost no difference to the confidence intervals. Even from a tiny universe, such as MPs (just over 600), the 95 per cent confidence interval for our value of 30 per cent from a 200 sample, only drops from ±6 per cent to ±5 per cent.

Formulating the questions to ask

There is a good deal of skill involved, but not much magic, in drafting an effective questionnaire. A lot of this is common sense; you do not ask for spontaneous awareness of universities right after questions relating to the Boat Race. The structure generally works best going from the general to the specific, and you do not ask leading questions. Here is a lovely one used by Gallup in 1938: 'Are you in favour of direct retaliatory measures against France's piracy? – Yes/No'

It is good to mix up types of questions in order to avoid respondent boredom or fatigue, and there are frequently more ways than one to pose a question. For example, you could ask sixth-form students to rate various factors in importance (on a 1 to 10 scale) for their choice of institution. The trouble is that they may assign a 9 or 10 score to lots of items, so this form of questioning may not discriminate well. It might be better, and quicker, to ask them to select the *six most important*, i.e. to force them to make choices.

In some situations it is best to ask open-ended questions: 'why do you say that?'; in others, providing a list of options that people can tick is preferable; and if a more detailed consideration of an issue is required, then a question like, 'how strongly do you agree or disagree that . . . ?', may work best. It is always a matter of judgement, and this is another reason why you should involve professionals and benefit from their experience. (One tip: researchers rarely use yes/no questions, unless the questions relate to behaviour, e.g. did you go through clearing? Attitudes are better handled by a scaled response: how strongly/to what extent/what, if any? Most client briefs or drafts consist entirely of yes/no questions.)

Market research 'deliverables' ◼

With modern technology, market researchers can provide findings in many formats: raw data, computer tabulations, interpretive report, charts and graphics, formal presentations. You should discuss your requirements with the agency well in advance: it would be a waste of your budget and the agency's time to have a lengthy report which will just gather dust on your shelf. Many clients prefer a 'working debrief' session at which the findings and their implications are discussed by client and researcher, sometimes followed by an executive summary and supporting graphics.

Cost-effectiveness of market research ◼

This is difficult territory, since it involves making a judgement about the value of the research you have commissioned. This is rarely possible in purely financial terms, and what value do you place on having a better prospectus or knowing student views on residential accommodation? To some extent it is a circular argument: you would not have spent £20,000 on a study if you had thought it would not be worth it. But how do you know you could not have achieved nearly the same benefit for an expenditure of £10,000?

As ever, the solution comes back to making the best use of your research company. If you have discussed your requirements in detail with the potential supplier, the design should constitute an ideal balance between usefulness and cost. Listen to the agency's ideas for adding value:

- Incorporating a few additional questions on a related topic to expand the scope of the project; e.g. if you are carrying out a piece

of research primarily to establish the image of the institution among internal stakeholders, why not also ask a few questions related to job satisfaction?
- Using some identical questions to those used in another survey, or last time, so that comparisons give another perspective; e.g. how satisfied are your staff? How does their level of satisfaction compare with that of staff at other universities? Is it better or worse than previous surveys?
- Not asking 'nice to know' questions if they will add to cost.
- Reducing the sample size, where doing so does not significantly jeopardize reliability.
- Ensuring that the questions are posed in a way that will help you make key decisions better; e.g. if you find that students are dissatisfied with the quality of teaching at your institution, a follow-up question: 'why are you dissatisfied?' will provide information which can help you to improve the quality.
- Using the agency's knowledge of the subject material to sharpen the focus of the study.

Perhaps most important: do ensure you invest enough time and resources to making the best use of the data after the researchers have gone. Research is a means to an end, not an end in itself.

Further reading

Worcester, R. and Downham, J. (eds) (1986) *Consumer Market Research Handbook*. Amsterdam: ESOMAR.
Hutton, P.F. (1990) *Survey Research for Managers*. London: Macmillan.
The Research Buyer's Guide (annual). London: Market Research Society.
Stuart, A. (1984) The ideas of sampling. *Griffin's Statistical Monographs*. High Wycombe: Charles Griffin.

4

IMPRESS IN PRINT
Publications

Frank Albrighton and
Julia Thomas

The scene is any higher education institution anywhere in the world. A few are gathered together to discuss an idea. At first the idea is a tiny glimmer of light, but slowly it grows until eventually it is clear and bright, illuminating sharply the career prospects of all those present. They are agreed on how they must safeguard the idea. They will form themselves into . . . A CENTRE. But now they falter. They have the idea. They have the Centre. What should they do next? Suddenly they realize that they must follow the old tradition, handed down through many generations, and with one voice they look heavenwards and cry: 'We must publish a brochure!'

What an unkind exaggeration. But perhaps you recognize the rush into print whenever any kind of communications need is identified. As communications professionals, we should be able to stand back and take a more objective view. If an institution of higher education wants to communicate with one or more of its audiences, there are, nowadays especially, many alternative forms at its disposal. They all have some advantages and they all have drawbacks.

We think especially today about new media. The internet is ubiquitous and infinitely flexible. It can carry vast volumes of information and it is interactive. But it is also ephemeral and can be inaccessible: your readers have to come to you. A video provides powerful moving images reinforced by dialogue and music. It echoes television, the most arresting medium of all time. On the other hand, it is expensive and inflexible. Its delivery is uncertain. Face-to-face interviews and meet-ings are direct and benefit from human contact, but they are difficult to arrange and are not cost-effective.

The point is that all forms of communication have their advant-ages and their disadvantages and you should be careful to decide which is most appropriate for your current needs. There is no doubt that print is special. Our culture and language are peppered with references that confirm its pre-eminent position. We do not think something is finally settled until we 'have it in writing'. Seeing something in print gives it an authority and a durability that other forms of communication cannot match, even when its reliability is spurious, as in the case of a tabloid newspaper. And we describe the most ominous of communications as 'the writing on the wall'.

In higher education, there is also a powerful traditional culture surrounding publications. For centuries, books, bookishness, learn-ing and scholarship have all been inextricably linked. Reading and writing are what happens in an institution of higher education. So it is unsurprising that when we think of communicating the qual-ities and attributes of an institution of higher education, we should think instinctively of some form of published material.

When is it best to use a publication? Print is authoritative and, when informed by market research, is unique in allowing you to tailor information to match the institution's goals and to target the market needs very precisely. But it will be expensive to produce and distribute, will probably be out of date within months of publica-tion and will take up valuable storage space.

Look at the publication that every institution of higher education must have in one form or another: the printed undergraduate pro-spectus. A recent survey confirmed what we all know: that potential students regard the prospectus as the most valuable source of infor-mation about what an institution has to offer.[1] A short time ago we might have said the same about the postgraduate prospectus, yet, in the United States, a substantial proportion of potential applicants now use the web as their primary source of information on post-graduate opportunities.

The range of media available to support, supplement and even replace publications is becoming more wide-ranging. At the same time, education marketing is becoming more responsive to the needs of individual customers and groups. It is not enough to think of your brochure, annual report or fundraising literature in isolation. Before you start, think carefully about the communications mix – advertising, web, open days, personal communications – and how, or even if, a publication can play an effective part in it.

Most publications fall neatly into one of two categories: those which provide information for the internal audience of staff and students – programmes, syllabuses, directories of personnel, events listings – and those which are designed to promote the institution to an external audience – potential students, donors, alumni and so on. In many institutions, the web has already taken over from the printed word in the first category. This chapter is mainly concerned with what we could describe as promotional publications.

Market research is important in every area of external relations but nowhere more so than in the production of publications. Research should be used at every stage to test the initial idea, work out plans and then to validate the publication that is eventually produced. In what follows we talk about research as it might be applied to an undergraduate prospectus, or perhaps a course brochure, but the principles are applicable to any form of publication.

At Birmingham, we have been conducting systematic market research on the undergraduate prospectus and other publications for about ten years. Each year we learn something new but there are also some very clear, common themes that have given us confidence in the way we prepare our publications. These themes have also been tested by other institutions and by independent research and are now familiar to many publications editors. Some of the questions to which we now know the answers are as follows:

- *How important is the prospectus?* The prospectus is the single most important source of information. This is helpful to know, not so much in confirming that you must have a prospectus, but in ordering priorities of time and money. If you cannot afford anything else to promote your courses, you must have a good prospectus. Not far behind the prospectus are course brochures. This information can be especially important when advising an academic department, as there may be pressures to produce more exotic forms of publicity. That is fine as long as the basic information that an applicant needs about the programme is presented to them well and accessibly in a brochure.
- *What else is important?* For Birmingham, where we have problems with perceptions of the city whose name we bear, visits to the campus are particularly effective. We know from research with applicants who have visited several universities during the application round that visits everywhere are a powerful influence.
- *What should you include?* Information about the programme is most important, followed by the grades that students will need in order to get in. In the non-academic information, by far the most important question is, 'where will I live?', followed by, 'and what

kind of a job will I get afterwards?' Information about social life, bars, restaurants, sports and so on is important but it is clearly second-order in the decision-making process.

- *What should be the balance of information?* Academic information is by far the most important. Whatever students may say anecdotally, choosing a place for their higher education is a serious decision to be based on serious information, and they are looking for authoritative statements from the institutions they want to consider.
- *What about design?* The same is true: the design should convey the qualities of the institution it represents and present information in a serious-minded manner. Just because the readers are of a certain age does not mean that your prospectus should ape the conventions of a teen magazine.
- *What sorts of pictures?* High quality, many and informative. Use them to demonstrate things that words can only assert: the atmosphere of the campus, the modern facilities. Raise the expectation: could that be me?

Our emphasis on research does not mean that there is no scope for imagination and innovation. In the competitive environment especially, a good editor should be thinking of new ideas for every edition, especially for a publication like a prospectus that can so easily settle into a comfortable rut.

Recently, we thought that we would transform the appearance of the Birmingham prospectus. We had two ideas. One was to break away from the two-thirds A4 format that is used by the majority of institutions and perhaps try a larger format, reminiscent of high quality commercial promotional literature. Let us delight our readers, we thought, with something different, not even sticking to the metric A sizes.

When we tried out this on focus groups of potential students in locations across the country the idea was rejected flatly. 'Those big prospectuses look like school text books,' they said. 'We cannot stand institutions who try to be different for its own sake.' 'What we need is something that looks like a prospectus, feels like a prospectus and is a prospectus.' So the conservatism of the modern student echoes that of teachers of many years ago who first influenced the A5 size of the late and unlamented CVCP Standard Prospectus in order that they could accommodate it tidily on library shelves. The development of the two-thirds A4 was designed to maintain library neatness whilst giving editors and designers a bit more scope.

Our other bright idea was to do something startling with the cover. For several years the images on the Birmingham prospectus had been fairly predictable. We had had the images of students at work in laboratories, libraries and generally looking happy around the campus. But the principal image had been of the main buildings of the University which are grand red brick edifices. This was not accidental. It was based on repeated research with potential undergraduates who found that these images actually said a great deal. They said that here was what they regarded as a 'proper university', well established, standing for high standards and representing all that is best in British education.

Fair enough, we thought, but surely we could do something a bit more racy. To find out what the implications of that would be, we took half a dozen prospectuses and removed the name of the institution together with any logos or devices that would make them identifiable. We made these up into dummy prospectuses and showed them to some potential students in order to see what the design and the images alone would say to them, without the clue of the name of the institution.

One very striking cover had a young woman looking forward to a bright future somewhere in the distance. All the students found that it had considerable impact. They thought it was inspirational and probably came from an institution with an art and design bias. They guessed it was a new university 'shedding its polytechnic image'. Although these reactions were mostly positive, they were presumably not those intended by the well established research-led university that published the prospectus.

Another cover included a number of images of people, obviously from all ages and backgrounds. Some students liked the inclusive message that this conveyed. For others, it was a drawback. Thinking about academic standards, they thought the institution would be open to everybody, whatever their ability. In fact the institution concerned is one of those most frequently referred to as being difficult to get into because of its demanding entry standards.

The research was conducted independently by MORI and we had mixed feelings when we read its report. The Birmingham cover had been one of the most liked on display. It had all the messages about Birmingham that we would wish to communicate and, 'overall it represented a friendly university with a good reputation and good facilities'. The cover design was not 'broken', so we had to suppress our urge to fix it.

But views can change, sometimes quite rapidly. What was once right may no longer be so and it is important to test your publications frequently with different target audiences.

When you are testing ideas for your publication it is as well to discuss the different forms that the print might take. There are arguments in favour of a fully fledged prospectus, although some

UK institutions are moving towards the American model of a publication that is more of a 'view book', where the promotional material is separate from a more sober listing of programmes or, in US parlance, a catalogue. Other printed forms that have their adherents include folders and posters.

In this early stage of the publication's process it is important to decide your priorities. There is often a reluctance to break with convention and try new marketing techniques. This is fuelled by a fear, exploited by determined advertising salespeople among others, of departing from what the majority are doing. We feel comfortable producing a glossy poster to advertise a course because it is a tried and tested method. But is it? Lots of people do it but how many have actually tested the effect of a poster or even bothered to find out if it reaches the appropriate noticeboard?

The important thing is to spend your money wisely. There are many pressures to spend money because it feels as though you are doing something. The skill is to be self-confident and to plan your activity after a rigorous and objective assessment of your own market position, your target groups and your resources. If you are working on a shoestring budget and can barely afford a new course flyer, for example, consider whether a well presented, carefully targeted letter from the head of the department or an invitation to a special open day might be more effective than a poorly produced publication. One academic department was determined to produce a glossy recruitment brochure to rival that of their competitors even though their funds would only run to a very small quantity. As a result they rationed copies of the brochure and were forced to send most enquirers a photocopy of the original.

So you have been through all the preliminary considerations. You have done your market research. You have thought about distribution and you have got an adequate budget to do the job well. Now you have to put it all together. In producing any publication there are a number of issues to be considered.

Who is in charge?

Publications are a central part of an institution's marketing programme. Their planning and production – writing copy, commissioning and managing design, print and photography, production scheduling, indexing, interviewing and so on – require the skills and experience of a marketing professional. Putting together a good prospectus or annual report is no longer a case of cutting and pasting contributions from across the campus. The work should be coordinated by a skilled, and tactful, editor. This suggests that the publications editor should be a member of the marketing office, or its equivalent, so that he or she can contribute to and draw on the range of professional skills and techniques available there.

What about an editorial board?

Some professional editors have an instinctive scepticism about editorial boards. They see them as interfering and a hindrance to their professionalism. Probably the problem comes from the title 'editorial board', which suggests some self-important body making policy decisions. A self-respecting editor will not need that. He or she should have been given policy directions related to the purpose of the publication, not to its editing. But that does not mean that an editor, however good, can single-handedly produce any publication. You do need help and you do need advice.

The trick is to marshal the appropriate input from the appropriate people. For example, if you are writing a general description of your institution's finances you must be absolutely sure that you have everything correct. This will involve consulting your finance office and probably seeking their approval to your finished product. But the last thing you want is an article written in accountant's jargon. It is part of the editor's job to manage these relationships in order to extract the authoritative information needed without conceding control over the words. Then you should obtain validation of the description that the expert would never have dreamed of.

The point is one that comes up so often in external relations. In a sense, you do not represent the institution or the finance office or the academic director of the programme: you are there to represent the interests of the reader, the outsider, the person who wants to know. If you put their interests first then the publication will come out right.

Who is going to write it?

Perhaps the most difficult part of the production of any publication from a higher education institution, and one which is all too often undervalued, is the copywriting. How can you make your institution sound more distinctive than the hundred others, many of which offer very similar products? How many promotional brochures or prospectus entries still waste that important paragraph by beginning:

'The department of imagistics was established in 1952 and is one of the leading schools of its kind in the country'?

The answer, as always, goes back to research. Find out what your readers are really interested in. There is no evidence that under-graduate applicants care about the age of a department (or of its staff) or that such information conveys anything to them about the quality of the course. What they do want to read about is the content of the programme and what is distinctive about it.

Does this mean then that the best author is the person who will teach the programme? Almost certainly not. Sales literature for cars is not written by those who design and build them. It is written by the marketing department which has the job of presenting the *benefits* of the product to the potential customer. Our frequent failing in marketing educational products is that we talk about what we can do and why we are doing it, rather than how the customer will gain from the experience. That is a marketing job and one which should be done by marketing professionals. They are the ones who will have a clear idea of the corporate messages that are to be conveyed and will ensure that every sentence works towards the publication's objectives.

In spite of its many problems, the car industry may not suffer from one that affects higher education institutions. This is that the whole of the academic community is literate and articulate. Academic staff spend their lives writing about their subjects. Their professional reputations depend on their ability to describe what they are doing in ways which are authoritative and comprehensive. How, then, are you to suggest that this is not necessarily a training for writing a prospectus entry? It is difficult sometimes, but one way or another it is important to persuade colleagues that the marketing of academic products is different from the academic process itself. But do not let this become a confrontation. The best results will come from a productive partnership where you both make a contribution based on your own areas of expertise.

Design: I know what I like

Everyone is an expert. If you ask me to knock up the design for the cover of a course brochure, I could probably do it in an afternoon. I would use my word processor, find an appropriate template and have a happy time playing around with typefaces, expanding them, condensing them and interspersing them with clip art. I would apply shadows and underlines. I would have bold text and small caps. By the end of the afternoon, I would be very pleased indeed. If you and

I were working together on a project I would show it to you and probably you would like it too. We might even find that it won the approval of someone who had nothing to do with our scheme but who liked what we had done with our graphics.

And we would have created something that was absolutely worthless. It would be amateurish and full of mistakes that would cause any professional graphic designer to shudder. Graphic design is a highly professional business but is seriously undervalued, particularly, for some reason, in higher education institutions. If you are serious about managing external relations you must manage matters so that good quality professional design permeates everything that you produce.

This is made somewhat easier if the marketing department includes an internal graphic design service. Designers working in this context will not relinquish their professional standards but will acquire an understanding and a sympathy for the academic environment and be able to relate to the special needs of education markets. They will also learn how to work productively in partnership with academic colleagues.

An internal graphic design service will also be thoroughly imbued in the principles of your visual identity policy. It will not be necessary for you to spend time briefing outside designers and printers on how your logo has to be reproduced and why particular design and typographical conventions have to be followed. A particularly effective inducement to academic departments to use the internal design service will be that, contrary to when they use outside agencies, value added tax will not be payable on the design service work.

In addition to masterminding the overall visual appearance of the publication, a good design service will also take responsibility for commissioning new photography or the production of other illustrations to ensure that there is a high and consistent standard throughout the publication. The editor must ensure that *every* image supports the main messages of the publication. Pictures should be compelling, but not included for that reason alone. They must help to tell the story.

Sometimes, pictures are acquired from picture agencies and elsewhere. This can be one way to acquire pictures that are out of the ordinary, but it can be costly. A new point to bear in mind, and one upon which the marketing office will be briefed, is that recent data protection legislation in the UK applies to photographs of individuals in the same way as it applies to information about them. For this reason, newspapers, for example, are now far more reluctant to release photographs taken for their news pages for you to use in your promotional literature. Another important requirement is that you must always credit the photographer, even if you commissioned the work and own the transparencies or prints.

Who shall we get to print it? ∎

One of the truths about printers is that you can always find one who will do it cheaper. Printing is a fiercely competitive business and, although prices will be based upon time and materials, a printer quoting for a job may well offer an estimate that seems irresistible, especially if the firm has not worked for you before. There are a few things to look out for. One is that you must always be sure that you are comparing like with like. It is very easy for a printer to shave a little off a specification to make the price come down. A not-so-legitimate practice is to quote a low initial price and then to regain the position by adding on lots of 'author's corrections'. Print buying is an art and is another part of the publication process that is best left to the experts. If you are not experienced and are tempted to dabble, there is a danger that you will compromise the quality of the publication that you have worked so hard to produce. Different printers specialize in different types of work, but they may not always tell you so. It is possible that the person who is actually printing your work has nothing to do with the company you engaged but is a remote subcontractor. If the job does go wrong, you need to be fairly self-confident and knowledgeable to be able to complain about quality when faced with a smokescreen of technical reasons why it happened and why it was probably all your fault anyway.

The technical world of printing is changing fast. Digital printing is now a reality and has changed some of the ground rules about what will be expensive and what will not, and about the different stages and processes of proofs, prints and plates.

As a manager in the UK you should also be alert to the legal requirements of the European Union. If the total expenditure on print of your institution exceeds a certain amount (in 2000, £144k excluding VAT) then the EU requires that you should invite tenders from right across Europe. At first sight, this is a horrifying prospect, raising the possibility of having to have your little leaflet printed on the other side of the continent. Although this is another minefield, it is one that can be successfully negotiated with the help and support of your purchasing office.

The happy day arrives when your publication is delivered. If, in spite of all that proof reading by all those people, an error has remained in your publication, you can rest assured that you will now instantly spot it as large as life, as soon as you open the publication. But let us assume that all is well and you are ready to distribute your leaflet. If you follow the precepts of this chapter, you will know exactly where you are going to send it and have ready labels and packages for distribution. Even now you have to be vigilant. Some years ago when the new technique of shrinkwrapping parcels came on to the market, one institution embraced it with enthusiasm. This was seen as a wonderful way to dispatch prospectuses so that they would arrive in the applicant's home, glossy with great impact from the carefully designed cover. Imagine the dismay of the editor who received a telephone call from a railway official informing him that 'all your books have burst open on Peterborough station'.

This is not the end of the story. Publication is not the same as communication, and it is important to find out whether your publication actually worked. This is an objective question: does it do what we intended? It is nothing to do with people saying, 'I like it'. You will probably have observed the situation in which someone comments on a publication from another institution: 'I like it' means 'therefore it is good', which in turn is rapidly translated into 'we should have one'. This is not the way to plan publications, and whether you and your colleagues like them is no way to judge them. You must go back to the target audience, the reader. You must continue your research process to find out what they think of it. Even in their case, the like/don't like response is not really the critical one. You need to find out what effect the publication has on them and whether it influences them to act in the way that you would wish. Publications are not art and they are not about self-expression. They are marketing tools to be used to inform and influence opinions so that your target audiences act in ways which are beneficial to your institution.

Note

1 *Making the Right Choice. How Students Choose Universities and Colleges* (1999) Report by the Institute for Employment Studies to CVCP, HEFCE and UCAS. London: CVCP.

5

COMMERCIAL BREAKS
A planned approach to advertising

Cyrrhian Macrae

We have all been there. The telephone rings and an enthusiastic telesales person launches into all the reasons why you should advertise in their publication. Sometimes it is very easy to pick holes in their script; but sometimes their arguments appear to be convincing, even compelling. And if the truth were told, we have probably all fallen victim to pressurized advertising sales at least once too often. Some of us learn the hard way – a dissipated budget with nothing to show for the expenditure. One thing is certain: by making that spur-of-the-moment decision, we are not being strategic and our advertising is not forming part of a well thought out, considered plan.

We are all in the same situation: increasing competition from other higher education providers both at home and overseas and more and more demands on a marketing budget that barely keeps pace with inflation. So it is worth reminding ourselves that there are some basic steps that can be followed to help ensure that our advertising spend is targeted and brings about results. Brannan says that: 'Defining the right approach to advertising demands a planned approach; and that's the key to making it pay for itself'.[1] In other words, advertising is not an activity to be viewed in isolation. It has its place in your organization's planning process.

The starting point for effective advertising is your organization's corporate or business plan. Your marketing plan will, in effect, be

Table 5.1   Activities involved in a product launch

Activity	Purpose	Application in higher education
Advertising	To announce the product to a wide audience quickly	Launch of a new course
Direct mail	To focus on the most likely short-term hot prospects	To focus on the most likely short-term hot prospects
Seminars	To provide an opportunity to demonstrate the product	Open days; specialist talks at HE fairs, careers evenings
Sales promotion	To encourage early take-up	Through attendance at HE fairs, careers evenings etc., persuading prospective students to apply for the new course
Public relations	To spread the word on early successes	Press releases to targeted journals explaining benefits of the new course
Video and literature	To arm the salesforce and help them sell	To arm the salesforce and help them sell

After Brannan, T. (1993) *The Effective Advertiser*. Oxford: Butterworth–Heinemann.

a subset of the corporate plan. An essential constituent of the marketing plan is its communications section, which will set out the ingredients of your marketing mix. Advertising is not the only marketing tool available to you and will feature alongside public relations, attendance at exhibitions and fairs, direct mail and so on. It will be more effective when it is one of the ingredients within the marketing mix, and is supported by other activities.[2] The ingredients of the mix may vary from campaign to campaign but Brannan[3] suggests that, for a new product launch, a suitable approach might be as shown in Table 5.1. The third column has been added to demonstrate how this approach can be adapted to a higher education environment, planning for the launch of a new degree, for example.

Each element of the marketing mix needs to be considered carefully in order to assess its strengths and weaknesses. Sometimes it will be apparent what will be the most appropriate means of promoting your product. In other cases you will need to compare the cost-effectiveness of various means to reach your target audience and what added value a particular medium will offer.

An important factor in determining whether advertising is the right medium is the fact that there *is* a price ticket attached to it. You are paying for the accuracy of your message and the way in which it is being conveyed. Furthermore, advertising offers the added benefit of delivering your message to a large audience, all of whom will receive the message within approximately the same timescale.

Effective advertising ▪

The effect of advertising on the target audience has been the subject of many debates over the years. Mass communication research shows that direct effects are at best limited.[4] In fact, it is generally held that, if anything, society is extremely sceptical of specific messages conveyed by advertising. The hypodermic syringe model of information being injected into a susceptible audience has long been dismissed. It is no good assuming that there is a passive audience of prospective students sitting out there, just waiting for you to tell them what course they should study. Where a lifestyle image is being sold, however, it does appear that advertising is more successful. For example, a student looking for a busy social life or part-time work is more likely to be influenced by an advertisement that points out the benefits of a city-centre campus. An advertisement may reinforce what individuals already believe rather than changing their attitude altogether.

According to Brannan,[5] the golden rules for effective advertising are that it should:

- get attention
- be relevant
- be clearly branded
- have consistency
- answer 'what's in it for me?'

Selecting the right media for your advertising is a key factor in the production of effective advertising. Is local commercial radio the answer? Would TV advertising be more appropriate? Would a local evening newspaper be more successful than a regional daily? Let us take local radio as our example. Most of us have a choice of commercial radio stations available to us – and with the arrival of digital media our choice will be even broader. Find out what the station's audience profile is before determining whether to place your advertisements with it. For example, one radio station may be better suited to part-time course recruitment advertising because its audience profile is aged 25–55, whereas another with an audience profile of 15–25 is better suited to full-time recruitment opportunities.

There is a plethora of publications aimed at the 15+ age group, which go direct to schools and colleges. They are often glossy, well produced, attractive – and expensive. But the very fact that there are so many of them and that new titles seem to be added with monotonous regularity will cause most marketing colleagues to take stock. Often a sale is made direct to a colleague in a department or faculty who has been swayed by the persuasive salesperson. Whilst you might fear that they are wasting their money, you need to be able to back up your argument with facts. If your advertising agency has a number of higher education clients, it may well have conducted research amongst target age groups to gauge the importance of particular sources of information. If they have not, suggest that they do. Or, you could always run focus groups amongst attendees at open days or amongst first-year students in your own institution to see how they narrowed down their choices. This is the sort of evidence you need to support your 'hunch' about the value of respective publications.

In addition to this advice, there are some other steps that can be taken that will improve the effectiveness of your advertising. Research has a very significant part to play.

The role of research

Advertising guru David Ogilvy says: 'Advertising people who ignore research are as dangerous as generals who ignore decodes of enemy signals.'[6] Jefkins tells us to regard research as a form of insurance against wasting money on ineffective advertising, and as a means of monitoring the effectiveness of a campaign while it is running and after the campaign has ended.[7] You will probably be in full agreement with the sentiments expressed above, but view with some trepidation the prospect of having to extend the already overstretched resources in your marketing team even further. Before you rule it out, see if your advertising agency can help you. It may cost you a little more money, but that should be offset by the benefits of a much better campaign. Your agency should have at its fingertips the expertise and resources to carry out the appropriate research, as well as the ability to analyse results.

In an ideal world, there are three research phases: pre-campaign, research to be conducted during the campaign, and testing once the campaign has finished.

Pre-campaign

You need to know what motivates your market. Desk research – the information available from published sources, either printed or electronic – is invaluable in providing a broad overview of market size and trends. Take the prospective undergraduate market, for example. There is also national research available such as *Making the Right Choice*, which demonstrates what factors figure highly in a prospective student's decision-making process.[8] But there may be local factors that come into play as well, so carry out your own research and consider the two alongside each other. Knowing what is important to your audience will affect the approach you take to copy and to creative ideas. It may also affect your choice of media.

Testing should begin at an early stage in the development of creative concepts. The first step is to select your proposition and your theme. Focus groups of first-year students can help immensely when planning a clearing campaign, for example. Their application and admissions experience is still fresh in their minds. They can tell you what mattered to them in that pressurized period following publication of A-level results. You can show them competitors' advertisements as well as your own and see what themes emerge in terms of likes and dislikes, choice of colours, use of visuals and graphics, and appropriate media. You may want to show them a previous year's campaign by way of comparison. But a word of caution: if you are showing them the concepts for this year's campaign, make sure you show them the concepts for last year rather than the 'finished article'. They need to compare like with like or they are sure to select the idea that appears more complete, more developed. The other thing to bear in mind is that the people on whom you are testing your advertising are not advertising specialists. What you are trying to gauge is their reaction to the ideas, not their assessment of the advertising itself. The true worth of this sort of pre-testing is that poor ideas will be weeded out.

Next, you need to be sure that the way in which your message is treated creatively actually aids understanding amongst your target audience, rather than hinders or obscures it. Make sure the headline works. Is it eye-catching? Ogilvy is very clear on this point: 'On average, five times as many people read the headlines as read the body copy. It follows that unless your headline sells your product, you have wasted 90 per cent of your money.'[9] He goes on to reflect that the headlines that work best are those which promise the reader a benefit. Research into copy and creative ideas should be carried out before too much expense has been incurred – particularly important if it is a high-cost television campaign.

Research during the campaign

This is an area that is often neglected. Few of us, for example, run television campaigns that we can test in one region before assessing the campaign's effectiveness. With press advertising, a simple and effective test to carry out is next-day recall. And of course, we will all be able to measure an increase in activity – for example, requests for information on a conference that we have advertised or calls to a hotline – as our campaign progresses. By asking callers where they heard about the conference or the hotline number, we can obtain invaluable data that will help inform the next campaign. But re-member: in-campaign monitoring research must be planned as an integral part of the campaign before it starts.

Research after the campaign

Once your campaign is over, measure the outcomes – total number of enquiries received, or prospects that turn into real conference bookings, or real orders, or real customers. You can then work out the cost-effectiveness of the various media in which you placed your advertisements. Make sure you have planned well enough ahead so that the data collected are amenable to different analyses – you cannot stop and start again.

How to plan a campaign ∎

Let us now try to bring together some of the elements described above and plan our campaign.

Step 1

The first step is to analyse the current situation. Do an analysis of your organization's advertising over the past few years. Have a look at where advertisements were placed. Try to ascertain why particular media were chosen. Consider the messages that your advertising has carried. What mechanisms were put in place to assess whether it was successful or not and what did they tell you? Were any qualitat-ive measurements carried out? Whilst advice in textbooks is often directed towards large private sector organizations, do not ignore the importance of research.

Step 2

Next you need to ask yourself what you are trying to achieve. Be clear about your objectives and do not do anything without quantifying them ('I want this campaign to attract 30 per cent more callers to our course enquiry hotline over a two-week period'). It is a hard discipline, but one that pays enormous dividends. Your need to be able to measure the results properly, which means you have to build in from the start some sort of response mechanisms that will enable you to gauge whether the advert has had the desired effect. Measuring the effect of advertising is an inexact science, and the temptation is to neglect it, but unless you set benchmarks and targets, how can you decide where to direct your advertising spend on future occasions and how much to spend?

Step 3

You need to be very clear who is your target audience – and what it is that motivates them. Some advice from Corstjens will ring true to those working in higher education: 'Targets of any group of closely competing brands are going to cover largely the same group of people. If the targets are literally defined by "who" (actual physical group) they will all be exactly the same. The real differences in brands' targets has to be the different feelings or attitudes in the (same) people's heads.'[10] Or, in Ogilvy's words: 'Do not, however, address your readers as though they were gathered together in a stadium. When people read your copy, they are alone.'[11]

Step 4

Deciding on your message is very important. We have all seen adverts where the individual footing the bill has undoubtedly tried to get their money's worth – a multitude of messages strung together in an incoherent fashion. Resist the temptation – and persuade others to do the same. Focus on one, clearly defined message or proposition, the purpose of which is to persuade the reader, listener or viewer to respond in the way in which you want them to. According to Brannan: 'the best advertising not only has a message, it has a single, single-minded and simple one'.[12] When defining this single, single-minded and simple proposition, ask yourself what makes it unique, or better than your competitors', or improved. What is it that makes it stand out? How does it tie in with your marketing objectives?

Step 5

Final selection of media is the next step in the process, although this is something that will have formed part of your thinking from the outset of your campaign planning. To a certain extent it may be determined by the sort of advertising you are doing. It is important not to regard media selection as a bolt-on at the end – it is a key component of your advertising strategy. Appropriateness is the key word. What is the right medium for what you are trying to achieve? Is it radio? Is it print-based? Would television be better? Will it reach your target audience? Is there any added value to be obtained, for example an opportunity for editorial and photographs to supplement a paid-for advertisement?

Setting your budget ▮

Advertising is an expensive business, and none of us can afford to throw money away on advertising which is unplanned. We have to be absolutely clear what are our objectives and be as certain as we can be that our advertising will help us to achieve those objectives.

So now to that thorny question of how much you should be spending on advertising. The difficulty with this task is one on which all the textbooks are agreed.[13] There is no magic formula, but there are some useful approaches to consider. Taking last year's budget and adding a little extra for inflation might seem like a good way forward, but it is not the answer in the competitive world of higher education. So what useful methods might we consider?

We could establish a budget as a predetermined percentage of predicted sales, a model often used in the industrial market. One danger with this approach is that it is not necessarily going to reflect what needs to be done in order to meet our pre-set objectives. Alternatively we could decide to invest a certain amount of advertising spend according to each new student won, for example, with the budget being adjusted in line with the number of students who apply to us. Or we could try to estimate what our competitors are spending. Some data are available.[14] Once we know what our competitors are spending in relation to their share of the market, we can apportion a corresponding percentage of our budget according to the size of our own market share. But beware of using competitor spend as your only benchmark. Whilst you might be able to calculate their advertising spend, you will not be privy to all the other components of their communications plan. Then there are modelling packages on the market that you could use. These attempt to predict sales responses to changes in advertising expenditure. Another approach is to take just one element of our existing plan and leave it out, or change it, and then try to measure the effect. But as with all of the above, there is a 'health warning' attached to this approach: the perceived effect may be completely unrelated to your change in approach.

Before you despair completely and decide that the tried and tested method of 'the same as last year with a little bit for inflation' is the best approach after all, look at what is available to you. Firstly there is your experience and knowledge of the higher education market. Let us not underestimate that. Then there is your knowledge of the overall financial health of your own organization. It is no good coming forward with grandiose plans for advertising spend if your budget is about to be cut. You will have advertising expenditure figures available to you that cover the past few years and will probably have carried out some measurement of the effectiveness of your advertising spend, particularly for any big campaigns that you have run. So you will have some idea of which elements of a campaign worked and which were less effective. If you can isolate information relating to the number of calls you received during clearing for example, as a result of using Teletext or one of the national broadsheets, then you have valuable information to hand. By all means investigate competitor spend – but treat it with the caution it deserves as outlined above. And do not forget to add your original advertising objectives into the equation, calculating what sort of budget will enable you to meet those objectives and reach your target audience.

Achieving value for money

Experience shows that the easiest way to achieve value for money is to say no to unsolicited calls from telesales people. But it is also important to persuade colleagues across the institution with devolved budget responsibility to plan their advertising spend more carefully. This is something returned to in the next section.

Working with a good, reliable advertising agency is one way of achieving value for money. Value for money embraces much more than just how much an advertisement costs. Anyone who enjoys a good working relationship with an agency will know the benefits that such a relationship can bring. The agency can, in time, become an extension of your own work area, part of a valuable team available to help achieve your objectives. Moreover, an agency can save you money through the purchasing power that it is able to exert. The agency will help protect your organization's integrity through the production of consistent, quality-driven messages. It will save you money by negotiating deals on your behalf, and by obtaining extensions to unrealistic deadlines. It will take the hassle out of production and delivery, ensuring that the advert reaches its destination on time and in the correct format. And the length of time it can take you and your colleagues to come up with a snappy headline or creative concept can often be halved by the agency team. It is also worth remembering that, through their experience of other clients, whether in higher education, industry or the professions, the agency will often have a proven solution to a situation that is new to you. But again, a word of warning. It must be a good agency. The working relationship must not be allowed to become too cosy; you must not become too reliant upon them; ensure that the promises made about value for money during their selection process are maintained; go out to tender regularly and make sure that new ideas are brought to your account.

A uniform approach

Have you ever opened a newspaper and seen two adverts from the same institution that bore little resemblance to each other? The perception given is of an organization that portrays different and confused messages to its publics. Strategic advertising means that all parts of the organization need to sign up to its overall marketing objectives. The corporate marketing department needs to have overall control over how the organization is portrayed even if there are devolved budgetary areas within it. That does not mean that your colleagues throughout the institution should have no say in where they place their advertising: their specialist knowledge is of great importance. But it should be a partnership. You need to explain to colleagues the benefits of a corporate approach, including the quality of product and clarity of message. It may be a long, slow process bringing your colleagues on board, particularly if this represents a complete change. The production of cross-organization marketing plans, produced jointly between the central marketing function and locally can help enormously. In this way there can be a shift in the way in which colleagues regard advertising, no longer seeing it as the only resource available, to be used as a panic measure, but as just one tool available within a strategic armoury.

Conclusion

The type of approach adopted towards advertising in higher education has changed dramatically over the past five to ten years, as

6

CASTING YOUR NET
The Internet and its role in
education marketing

Michael Stoner

By about 2010 the Internet will have become the single most important channel by which colleges and universities market to their entire range of constituencies. This trend parallels two other inexorable trends: the emergence of web-based business processes and the use of the web in teaching and learning. All three trends are so important and will have such a great impact on the way that institutions work and market their work that they cannot be considered separately – at least not for very long. With its capacity to communicate quickly, conduct two-way transactions in real time, and facilitate access to otherwise separate databases, the web forces institutions to think across media, to plan across departments, and to market themselves – and to work – differently. This dynamism is particularly apparent in the management of external relationships.

Thinking across media

As important as the Internet will be in marketing an institution, however, it will always be just one component of an institution's communications and marketing strategy. Yet, one of the realities of institutional relations at the turn of the millennium is that websites and other Internet communications are often developed without a clear idea of how they relate to other communications – print, public relations, advertising – or an understanding of their role in a larger institutional marketing strategy. In order to create effective Internet communications, institutional leaders must first understand clearly an institution's communication and marketing challenges and then develop a multifaceted, sophisticated, long-term communications strategy.

In all cases, strategy depends upon knowledge of what the market requires. In the case of web development aimed at institutional marketing, this means research with external constituencies who interact with the institution supported by web development that meets their needs for information and access to institutional services and products. Oftentimes, the web can be a solution to the communications needs of internal audiences as well.

Meanwhile, audiences are shaped by daily exposure to the Internet, just as they have been shaped by use of more traditional communications. An increasing number of users, particularly those in America and the UK, have high expectations for web design and service. Meeting or exceeding those expectations will require an entirely new approach to institutional marketing. One of implications for college and university marketers is that they must begin managing their institution's Internet communications as if all their important constituents are using the Internet, because they soon will be.

In the United States, 35 per cent of youth aged 10–17 use the Internet 'almost every day' and for many of them, instant messaging is replacing the telephone as the preferred after-school way to communicate with friends.[1] Many of these teenagers attend college, where they are immersed in an information-saturated environment facilitated by high-speed Internet connections in classrooms, laboratories and residence halls. They leave campus and begin working in government and in information industries where a large amount of their daily business is conducted online.

The roles that the Internet already plays in campus life will be magnified when large segments of the public become wired and begin using the Internet in all aspects of their daily lives. This is already happening in the United States. By April 2000, research revealed that 60 million Americans go online in a typical day. And despite claims to the contrary, people say that use of the Internet actually enhances their relationships and enriches their lives: 55 per cent of Net users say email has improved their connections with family.[2]

Even more telling, this same study found that, every day in the United States:

- 52 per cent of Net users do something on the web
- 52 per cent of Net users send or read email

- 19 million people get news from the Internet
- 10.4 million people send instant messages
- 4.3 million people bank online.[3]

This means that the Internet is becoming a part of people's lives. And as faster connections to the Internet proliferate, it will become even more solidly entrenched as people use the enormous and growing wealth of information and services at their fingertips.

Not surprisingly, given these numbers, the Internet is playing an important role in student recruitment in the United States. In ongoing research with high school juniors and seniors, students indicated that the web was the third most important source of information about a college or university, ranking below a visit to campus and virtually equal to a talk with a current student.[4] On many campuses, alumni are becoming increasingly vocal about the need for services – many of them based on common Internet tools such as email, chat, and web services – all bespeaking a deeply felt desire to connect in many ways with a beloved alma mater and with each other. And the web is playing a more important role in fundraising, as universities follow the lead of non-profit organizations such as the Red Cross, which raises substantial funds through its website.

Given the fact that the Internet will play such an important role in recruiting, alumni relations and in philanthropy, the commitment to the Internet must be an institutional one, not merely the project of a single department. Institutions must develop a strategy for developing, managing, and maintaining their Internet communications as well as the kind of budget allocations and staffing that will create real, ongoing, robust and effective Internet communications completely integrated with other communications strategies. To begin, however, leaders must recognize the important role that technology will play and they must energize their staffs to utilize the technology effectively.

Promoting a culture of change

Part of the reality of managing in the information age is that technology will continue to advance quickly, that no one will ever be able to keep up, and that since there is no chance that anyone can keep up, there is little use in being anxious about it. The challenge is to recognize which technologies are useful and to adopt them, planning for their integration into office procedures, while being aware of possibilities presented by emerging products and processes. That requires keeping up with technology development and promoting a culture of change within the institution.

Leaders must create an internal climate that welcomes change, since change will be constant – in fact, the pace of change will probably accelerate. (This is what is known in industry as Internet time.) Although campuses have been largely immune to the fast pace of Internet development, that is likely to change as board members, alumni, funders and governments become more demanding of on-campus professionals. Managers must demonstrate their interest in, and be leaders in the use of, new technologies and the benefits they may bring to the organization. Of course, leaders must simultan-eously balance the hype ('everyone will be accessing their email through their cellphones and surfing the Net from PDAs') with the reality that many technologies take years to percolate down from the early adopters to a scale of use where they really matter on an institutional level.

One way that leaders can keep pace with development, promote a culture of change, and manage staff effectively is to develop an in-house technology group that can help to evaluate and implement new technologies. The group should be composed of staff members who are particularly interested in technology. The group should play an important role in new advances in technology and tracking these developments to see how they might affect the way you do business or relate to your various important constituencies. A staff group could be augmented by a small number of alumni, academics, or friends of the institution, who can bring a much-needed external perspective to group discussions and recommendations.

Department budgets must also include funds for training and staff development. This is essential as staff members expand their know-ledge and understanding of technology and how it can be used to further institutional goals. Training is an ongoing need: staff members will need to learn new skills, new processes and new technologies as they develop. Many campuses offer inexpensive training opportunit-ies, as do external organizations.

Finally, everyone must learn to work with colleagues in new configurations. Because the Internet crosses functional boundaries, the model of top-down management is breaking down. For example, staffing on web development projects is increasingly configured as a team that may include people from many departments sharing information and responsibility while a project is under way. Staff need help in understanding this model and developing the skills necessary for being an effective team member. Supervisors need assist-ance in understanding how to influence team-mates who do not report directly to them.

Developing a website that markets the institution effectively ■

Using the web as an effective tool in an institutional marketing and communications strategy depends upon a thorough understanding of the perceptions of the institution in the marketplace. Only then can an institution develop a plan that includes the use of the web, email, chat and other technologies in addition to print and other media. For instance, a personalized postcard may direct prospective students to a website; an article in an alumnus publication may rely on a scheduled chat session to bring alumni together online; a series of public radio spots on a significant campus topic may be supported by a website with specially developed content.

In order to fulfil such communications strategies, institutions must first ensure that their websites and other Internet communications are appropriately managed and that the main website can support the needs of the many outsiders who will seek information there. This is a significant challenge.

Too many institutions still view their websites as a source of information for on-campus users and do not make them easy for outsiders to navigate. However, as campuses develop robust intranets – enabling students, academics and administrators to log on and gain access to databases and the rich array of information that they need to do their jobs – the home page and site organization must evolve. For example, as the campus intranet becomes increasingly sophisticated and services are password-protected, the home page becomes primarily a tool for those who are not as familiar with the campus: alumni, prospective undergraduate and postgraduate students, research partners, and others. They will use it to find the information they need, so they must be able to grasp the site's organization quickly and move around the site with ease. As a result, home pages that organize information by audience needs help to channel members of those audiences to information that is of primary interest to them. Similarly, a well developed search function that can search the entire site is essential.

Just as important is a consistent site interface. There are several reasons why this is necessary. First and most importantly, a consistent look and feel coupled with a consistent navigation scheme ensures that visitors know where they are at every moment during their exploration of the site. Second, a consistent interface ensures that a visitor does not have to relearn how to use the site with each click. Third, a consistent interface ensures that the institution can maximize opportunities to reinforce its brand and positioning to visitors to the site.

In an age in which so many relationships will be mediated by the web, an institution's brand will take on extraordinary significance. This is as true in education as it is in business. All education institutions must focus on developing and extending their brands, ensuring that their messages are consistent across the media they use to market the institution. This is increasingly true *because* of the web. Even in 1980, one audience segment (i.e. prospective undergraduate students) seldom saw communications developed for another audience segment (i.e. alumni). Now, though, the web essentially invites side-by-side comparison, making inconsistency in branding and messages painfully apparent.

This is not to say that a website for alumni should duplicate the one for prospective undergraduates. The sophistication and information needs of various audiences differ, as does their comfort with various technologies. For example, alumni and older users are often much more security-conscious than prospective students. Young people in the United States are much more comfortable using instant messaging and chat than are adults.[5] Older alumni may feel uncomfortable using chat, so online community-builders working with them may need to use email more extensively than with younger alumni.

Prospective students may also be more alert than alumni regarding how effectively colleges market themselves online. Research with prospective students of American colleges and universities indicates that prospective students are not only keenly aware of the shortcomings of institutional websites but are critical of an institution's failure to present a distinctive image on its website. They cite this failing – as well as a lack of information about admissions and financial aid – as one of the most common shortcomings of college websites.[6] They also look at the alumni area of the site to learn if an institution really cares about people and works to maintain relationships with them after they have left campus.

Other applications for the web: business processes and learning and teaching

The web will do far more than market a college or university. Much campus business will be conducted via the web, as will a significant amount of learning and teaching. Institutional business processes facilitated by use of a sophisticated campus intranet are under development at universities around the world. The University of Delaware in the United States was a leader in developing what has come to be called a web-enabled campus. This means that members of the campus community, whatever their role, can manage their business with the institution and with other community members using a web browser as a link to many different sources of information across the campus. For example, administrators can file travel reports by using Netscape Navigator or Internet Explorer to link with a web form, complete it online, and file it by clicking a Submit button. Students can change their addresses and register for classes online. Academics can follow the progress of their students by linking to a class registry on the web.

As simple as these concepts are, they have powerful customer-service and marketing implications. These systems allow people all over campus to conduct their business at times and places convenient to them rather than rushing to a campus office at certain times of the day. The institution's 'customers' can avoid queues, and in some situations they feel that a computer is fairer than humans can be (in lotteries for oversubscribed classes, for example). One can easily see the advantages of these systems, since they resolve many of the long-standing complaints about routine business transactions that have plagued many campuses.

However simple and compelling these concepts seem, they are often technically difficult to put into practice. Developing these types of systems requires rationalizing campus databases and systems and building software that links sources of information to users. Depending on a variety of variables, this can be quite complicated and require a large investment. Not all institutions are prepared for this complex planning or budgetary commitment. And those are the easy parts of the project. Dealing with the consequences to the institution's human systems and encouraging staff to adapt to new technologies or procedures is even more difficult, although an essential component of the process.

For marketers, however, there are incredible opportunities to be found here. As institutions are able to collect and retain information about web visitors, mining databases becomes an important way to link audiences with information that is of interest *to them*, making personalization of websites and one-to-one marketing a reality. Websites of businesses like Amazon.com already have the capability to link customers to a database that tracks their purchases and allows the company to provide an increasingly personalized stream of information, all of it geared to selling more products. Less exotic, but equally compelling, is the fact that excellent web-based student services provide a differentiating factor in the marketplace: already, many American campuses position themselves as 'wired' or '24–7'.

The role of e-commerce

Developing e-commerce capabilities will also be vital in order for institutions to function in a networked world. Becoming part of the Internet economy involves being able to accept online transactions, currently primarily achieved through credit cards. Yet most institutions have difficulty with credit card transactions. Many university and college economic models do not accommodate the costs of processing credit card fees and most campuses do not have or cannot manage a secure server. Few external vendors offer an integrated solution for credit card processing for colleges. As a result, most institutions in the United States develop e-commerce strategies in a piecemeal fashion. One vendor may provide an online application to the admissions office and process credit card transactions as a service to applicants. Another vendor may develop the website for the athletics department and process credit card payments for online ticket sales for sporting events. Still another vendor may service the fundraising office, allowing donors to give online and processing their transactions. And a fourth vendor may serve a key postgraduate division that recruits internationally and requires credit cards for its foreign applicants.

Business officers will soon realize that their institutions are not being well served by this fragmented strategy and will seek economies of scale to reduce credit card processing fees and ensure an appropriate level of security for these important transactions. And marketers will soon realize that a well developed, well implemented e-commerce strategy is as important to them as it is to the financial officers. An institution's audiences will expect to be able to buy an array of products and services from universities, as they do from retailers and financial service institutions and other web businesses. And they will ask, why, if they can manage their bank account online and pay bills through the web, they cannot pay for their tuition in the same way.

Learning and teaching

The core business of a university or college, of course, is education. And it is much easier for many institutions to understand the value of such initiatives as web-enabling information management and rationalizing online payments than it is to envisage just how the various available technologies will facilitate learning and teaching. This is in part due to the very slim bandwidth that will continue to be available to at-home users for some time to come, making streaming video to home users out of the question.

Class websites that contain the reading list, lecture notes and other materials for classroom work; the use of email for student–faculty interaction; learning interactions facilitated through chat; lectures delivered by video; robust collections of learning resources (artworks, texts, videos and other material): all these can now be available online, 24 hours a day, seven days a week. In this form, they augment face-to-face student–faculty interactions on many campuses. Their use will only grow as teachers and academics become more adept at understanding how to package and deliver these materials using the web and as institutions provide the resources to academics to help them do that.

Beyond these obvious supplements to current teaching and learning practice is a multiplicity of experiments aimed at understanding the advantages and disadvantages of learning and teaching mediated by technology. Some faculty that I have interviewed say that, as much as they believe technology can enhance the learning experience for their students, integrating even simple technology such as email into their teaching imposes a greater burden because it creates a much higher level of interaction with students. This takes time away from their other activities, such as their own research, and suggests to them that online learning may be even more demanding (and therefore expensive) than traditional lecture-based teaching.

The promise of software that enables students to learn while doing – sophisticated simulation-based teaching or the various products that model scientific processes – *could* revolutionize the way students learn. However, such software will be expensive to develop. Furthermore, many academics, evaluated primarily on the quality of their published research, may be hesitant to engage in developing such tools unless their institutions reward them financially and allow their evaluations to be based in part on these activities.

In any case, the real benefits (and drawbacks) of technology-mediated learning and teaching will be understood only over the long term. There is much opportunity to experiment with various models when delivering education on campus or to well-wired corporations and businesses. However, institutions which serve individuals in online learning programmes will continue to face the problem of limited bandwidth to the home and therefore serious limitations on the amount of information that can be delivered online.

Developing strategies for using the web effectively

Because the web will undergird so many facets of institutional life, crossing traditional boundaries, it is essential that strategies for planning, developing and extending it rely on input from people from across the institution. Leaders must encourage, and demand, cross-department cooperation and collaboration that seeks to further the interests of the institution, not just individual departments or groups. Politics too often impede the progress of projects that will benefit many people at the institution and many external audiences. For example, discussions of site architecture, organization and interface design invariably raise the issue of who should be managing an institution's website. In my view, which is informed by many years spent advising dozens of institutions on new media strategy and web development, the responsibility for developing an institution's strategy for its *public* website should be led by its chief marketing or communications officer. But information technology staff play an essential role in such activities, since they will be developing or supporting key aspects of this initiative, including both hardware and software. In addition, they may be managing the activities of many vendors needed to realize various elements of the strategy. And although the chief financial officer, too, has a crucial role in developing an e-commerce strategy, implementation of this strategy (as well as lack of a strategy) has implications for institutional marketing.

Similarly, academics must lead the discussions in developing learning and teaching initiatives, but marketing staff have a role to play here. For example, for online learners, the web will be the primary focus for interaction, and institutions will compete by showcasing quality web-based services. Marketers must be involved in packaging courses and creating activities that enhance the relationships of online learners with each other and with the institution. Universities must not miss the opportunity to reinforce the values of the institutional brand and to extend it to those alumni who attend the virtual campus.

The Internet will change many things about the way institutions communicate and do their business. Fundamentally, though, it is just a technology, albeit a powerful one, and its primary role will be to mediate relationships. Harnessing the power of the Internet will enable people to be involved in new kinds of relationships with institutions. In some cases, these will be short-term learning relationships, but the promise of the Internet is far more powerful than that.

One primary example is that the Internet allows members of external audiences to be involved in the life of an institution in ways never before possible. The opportunities are perhaps more obvious for alumni than for other groups, since these people already have a relationship with the institution and often wish their connection to their alma mater to be deeper and richer than it is. The interactive nature of the web allows alumni to be involved in the life of the institution in many new ways: mentoring students without having to be on campus, providing input into issues of alumni or even institutional governance, or taking classes are some of the clearer examples. This creates the possibility of a type of relationship marketing never before possible in an increasingly global society.

Notes

1 *Kaiser Family Foundation – National Public Radio Poll* (February 2000). Menlo Park, CA: Kaiser Family Foundation. Also at http://www.kff.org/ (accessed 2000)
2 *Tracking Online Life: How Women Use the Internet to Cultivate Relationships with Family and Friends* (May 2000). Washington, DC: Pew Internet and American Life. Also at http://www.pewinternet.org/reports/toc.asp? Report=11 (accessed 2000)
3 Ibid.
4 *Web Site Effectiveness Study*. Chicago, IL: Lipman Hearne. www.lipman hearne.com. Also at www.wses.com (accessed 2000)
5 In the United States, 59 per cent of Internet users between the ages of 18 and 24 use instant messaging and 53 per cent have used chat. Young people are also far more likely than adults to listen to music online (10 per cent claim to do it daily) and to use the web to find and download movie trailers and other video files. *Tracking Online Life*, op.cit.
6 *Web Site Effectiveness Study*, op.cit.

7

'HAPPY DAYS' OR 'NIGHTMARE ON FLEET STREET'?
Media relations

Peter Evans

The media – radio, television, newspapers, magazines and so on – is the way in which most people find out about what academics get up to. Research stories in particular are increasingly sought after, and people able to translate complex ideas at the sharp end of their discipline into the everyday language required by mass audiences are a valuable commodity. Should academics, though, become involved in media work – and, if they do, what can they expect from these interactions?

Consider this scenario. Dr X is a respected academic specializing in the changing political face of central and eastern Europe. One day she receives a call from the local radio station. At the suggestion of her university press office, the producer of a current affairs programme is asking Dr X to come along that afternoon to talk about 'The new Europe: what it means for us'.

Surprised, delighted and a little uncertain as to what exactly is wanted of her, Dr X straightaway agrees and, later that day, finds herself in the foyer of the radio station where a young programme assistant greets her. 'What are we doing, exactly?' asks Dr X. 'Oh, you know,' says the young man, 'it's just a chat about Europe and everything with our presenter, Steve. He's really nice.' Ten minutes later, Dr X is ushered into the studio for a live chat with Nice Steve. Also there is the Chair of a local residents' association, visibly in a state of some agitation. It quickly transpires that there is a problem in the neighbourhood with central European refugees who are, says Agitated Chairperson, 'begging in the streets and generally causing a nuisance'. Suddenly Dr X appreciates the situation – let us call it a dilemma – in which she finds herself. She has already been cast in the role, quite arbitrarily, of apologist for this 'refugee problem', simply because of her knowledge of the dynamics of east/west pan-Europeanism. It is an ugly moment, and she cannot wait to get out of that studio. On her way back to the familiar surroundings of her department, our luckless Dr X vows never again to meddle with the media.

Now, many academics believe that this sort of interaction is pretty typical. They are suspicious of the media on the grounds that its sole ambition is to distress, humiliate, misrepresent and generally upset those members of the academic world unfortunate enough to get mixed up in it. Are they justified in their mistrust, or is the story of Dr X a gross caricature? To answer those questions we need to look a little more closely at the media culture.

Uncertainties of the marketplace ■

This is a fierce marketplace. Organizations such as universities, learned societies and research councils are constantly trying to 'sell' stories to the media while, internally, reporters and producers have to sell ideas to their editor. Academically-derived stories have to compete with all the other events taking place – be they an earthquake, a mass exodus of refugees or a political scandal.

In order that a story can compete, it must have strong news characteristics. What is news? It is anything that is new, original, novel, unique, engaging, intriguing, counter-intuitive, funny, tragic – the list of adjectives is endless, but they all amount to one basic quality: relevance to the reading/listening/viewing public. There is also another important consideration. News is anything that an editor thinks it is. There are really no formulae. It is all very subjective, even whimsical.

Some programmes specialize in subject matter with an academic flavour such as scientific research. The reporter or interviewer may be a dedicated science/medicine correspondent. More often, though, you will meet generalists – people who cover a wide range of subjects – reporting one day on a physics or social sciences discovery, the next, on crop failure among hop growers. In fact, these two sorts of reporter – the specialist and generalist – are not so different as they might first appear. They both want you to make your story relevant to their audience, to bring your research down to a basic level.

If relevance to the audience is important, so too is 'colour' – drama, conflict, even disaster. The film *Apollo 13* shows that the US public was tiring of NASA's moon missions until a tragedy loomed. As audiences, we like drama. No newspaper would get many readers with a headline: 'Tall Building Remains Standing'. The international monetary system is very dull unless and until some computer whizzkid manages to swindle it out of billions of Euros. A flood, an air crash – these are the stuff of news. So it is really not at all surprising that editors might take an interest in a press release headed 'Possible new treatment for cancer', whereas 'Cell biologist characterizes interesting protein' would not capture much, if any, media attention, important though the discovery may be in scientific terms.

Whatever the circumstances, however, all media interactions represent an opportunity for scientists to tell their story. Normally, the procedure is proactive. A press release is issued telling the world that something new has happened. Occasionally, an organization and its researchers need to be reactive, picking up on an event in the news such as the collapse of a new, high-tech bridge. Even more occasionally, organizations are put on the defensive and have to react by 'firefighting'. On the surface, it seems as if these scenarios are different. In practice, one can ensure that they are quite similar, even turning what seems to be a damage limitation exercise into a vehicle for conveying positive messages.

The reason for this may surprise you. Most people believe – wrongly – that a media interview is driven exclusively by the reporter or interviewer. It is not. You the expert, the person with important and interesting things to say, can steer the interview. The interviewer, far from being a puppet master, is really only taking his or her cues from you.

What the interviewer really wants

Interviewers want a powerful story to seduce their audiences. They want this from the lips of a well informed and committed individual who appears keen to impart information in a stimulating and entertaining way. What interviewers do not want is: methodology, theory, all-inclusive technical explanations, academic or esoteric asides. You will find, constantly, that you will be asked, 'Why is this important?' – the ubiquitous 'So what?' question.

Interviewers will try always to get you to relate what you are talking about to their readers/listeners/viewers. The more you know about these audiences, therefore, the easier you will find it to convey your message. So listen and look carefully at the treatment of your kinds of story in the media. Note the kinds of question asked and think about what answers the interviewer is trying to elicit.

Almost invariably you will find that the interviewer wants to be on the same side as the interviewee. Many believe that the purpose of an interview is to maximize the discomfort of the interviewee and distort his or her messages. Nothing could be further from the truth. With the exception of political interviews, which are usually intended to challenge the interviewee on behalf of the public, alienation makes for a bad interview. If there is conflict and discomfort, then there will not be that smooth exchange of entertaining information that audiences want. Instead, you get a verbal boxing match.

Preparing for interviews ▉

If a newspaper or broadcaster approaches a researcher with a request for an interview, it is of value to ask some preliminary questions in order to prepare yourself. These are:

- What is the programme (newspaper/magazine) in which my contribution will appear? What can you tell me about your audience – their intellectual sophistication, age range, demographics?
- What format is the programme or article? News, magazine or feature style? How will you use my contribution? Will it be edited and set alongside other material? If so, where does that material come from?
- What ground are we covering? This is vital. You must agree on the areas of your work that you will be asked about. Many difficulties arise simply because an interviewee believes that he or she will be asked about topic A whereas the journalist wants to talk about topic B or C or even X.
- Is the interview live or pre-recorded? Many inexperienced interviewees prefer recorded interviews because they know that if they make a mistake, get tongue-tied or simply dry up, it is not a disaster. You stop the tape and start again. Others prefer live interviews because you can say exactly what you like. If you have good, strong, clear messages then you can state them and repeat them and no one can do much about it. This is why politicians like to take part in live broadcasts.
- Am I on my own or are you interviewing others at the same time in a discussion format? Who are the other contributors? You can readily see the importance of knowing this. A doctor, for example, may be called on to argue the orthodox scientific case against an advocate of complementary medicine. An atmospheric chemist

could well be asked to discuss ozone depletion along with an environmentalist, and so on. The more you know, the better you can prepare your case if advocacy is required.

- Where and how will the interview take place? In a studio? On location? In my office? Down a line? On the telephone? Novice interviewees prefer face-to-face interactions where you can see non-verbal cues. Line interviews can be disconcerting if you are not accustomed to doing them. You may feel happier too if a reporter or film crew comes to your lab or office where you are on home ground rather than in the strange surroundings of a studio. Again this is usually a matter of experience.

One word of warning about giving telephone interviews. The telephone is a familiar instrument, used every day to chat, discuss, impart confidences and so on. It is quite easy to say more than you intended to over the telephone, and to regret it afterwards.

One final matter to raise about a prospective radio or television interview might be, 'What questions will you ask me?' Certainly, 'What is your first question?' is useful. The big problem with asking for all the questions in advance is that there is no guarantee that the reporter will adhere faithfully to them. Interviewers are, if nothing else, good listeners. If, in the course of one of your answers, you say things that seem particularly interesting, you will usually be asked to clarify or amplify. In other words, the interviewer may, in the interests of the audience, depart from a strict sequence of questions. There has to be flexibility.

This may seem like bad news but it is quite the opposite. Suppose, for example, a pharmacologist agrees to an interview on the safety aspects of a new drug. It is easy to use this as an opportunity to draw attention to the immense importance of diabetes research or advances in incontinence treatments by putting out teasing little phrases about them that no interviewer can resist asking you to say more about. Think about what those tempting phrases might be for your area of research.

Once you have asked the broadcaster or journalist these preparatory questions and received satisfactory answers, you can proceed with the interview. If the answers are not satisfactory you may wish to think again about agreeing to take part.

Selecting your material

The average interview length on radio or television is around three minutes. You have just 180 seconds to get your messages across, so what are the two or three key things that you want to say? Make sure you have them fixed firmly in your mind. You will not be able to speak clearly and briefly unless you are sure about them.

In framing your answers remember the 'So what?' imperative. The general public cannot be expected automatically to be interested in research for its own sake. You need to give them a reason to be involved. Few of us are intrinsically fascinated by, for example, macro-economic theory or fiscal niceties, but we are very interested indeed in rates of personal taxation or the health of the world's stock markets because these topics bear directly on our everyday lives. You have to make the same bridges of relevance for your work.

Common problems

Often – not as often as you might think, but often enough – an interviewee ends the interview without having conveyed a clear message at all. One barrier is jargon or technicality. 'A bell-shaped Gaussian distribution' or 'hortative subjunctive' may well form part of your *lingua franca*, but try using those phrases outside your academic department and a look of incomprehension will spread across your listeners' faces. Yet those people are exactly the audience you have to keep in mind all the time you are putting your work into words for the media.

Numbers can cause problems too – size, distance, proportion and so on. People prefer 'about one in six' to '17 per cent'. They are uncomfortable with 'nanoscale', '10 to the 7', 'three microns across' and so on. Again, think of people in general and find ways of converting numerical ideas into more accessible language. Better than 'one part per 1000 billion' is 'one spoonful of water in an Olympic swimming pool'. So, be careful when putting numbers on risk. 'One in a million' or 'an 80 per cent chance' mean little to ordinary folk. Better to set these estimates in a telling context. 'There is less chance of developing this form of the disease than there is of seeing a UFO/winning the Lottery/finding gold in your garden.'

It is easy to assume that other people know the same things as you do – even what to you are quite mundane items of knowledge such as the components of a living cell, the fundamentals of the Constitution or the basic structure of higher education. Researchers from all disciplines tend to make this assumption: but whether it concerns protons, protozoa, proteins or post-modernism, basic knowledge is simply not in everyone's head. In an interview you may have to put it there or try to limit the amount of information you discuss.

Alongside errors of judgement about the intellectual or linguistic ability of the audience, come a range of more cosmetic errors: not what the interviewee says but how he or she says it. Do not forget that an interview is a social interaction, not a lecture or learned monologue. Allow your interviewer to react to what you are saying, especially if it is particularly exciting or novel. 'We have, for the first time ever, discovered something that points us in a very interesting political direction', needs a pause to allow the audience to take it in and the reporter to ask, 'What direction?' You can underline your message by asking your interviewer a question: 'We found a particular kind of chemical in the environment – and I wonder if you can guess why we were so excited?' simply begs the reporter to say, 'Tell me!'

Tone and style are important in interviews. A dull monotone is not consistent with exciting, valuable research findings. The declamatory style of some lecturers fits badly with the idea of a social chat that is being eavesdropped by listeners and viewers – which is what a good interview should be. A friendly, non-argumentative voice comes across far better than a tetchy 'boffin'.

Inexperienced interviewees can, understandably, become anxious and, when they do, they often make their answers too long. They try to fill the silence in the studio by chattering on long after they have made their point. Remember, it is the interviewer's job, not yours, to keep the interview moving along. If you finish your answer, even if it is a simple 'Yes' or 'No', then be quiet until the next question comes. Long answers are usually boring too.

The importance of pictures

All branches of the media – broadcast or print – deal in pictures, both real visuals but more importantly images created in the minds of the audience. As an interviewee you should fuel this need for graphic representation because pictures:

- allow you better to convey the complexities of your subject matter
- reduce the psychological distance between you and your audience
- leave something that resonates in the mind – a mnemonic for your messages
- entertain people.

Here are some of the ways in which pictures can be created:

- *Anthropomorphism* is a useful strategy. The late Peter Medawar once entertained an audience by suggesting that the cosmos may have been 'too reticent' to begin with a big bang. Primo Levi, industrial chemist-turned-author of *The Periodic Table* described stannous chloride as 'aggressive but also delicate, like certain unpleasant sports characters who whine when they lose' – thereby introducing a neat simile as well into his explanation. One of the classic pieces of anthropomorphism is that of Richard Feynman in a public lecture on neutrinos. 'These particular objects', said Feynman, 'do practically nothing at all except exist. You can use your son-in-law as a prototype.'

- *Similes* can be telling. 'The surface is thick and sticky like marmalade'; 'The molecule hops along like a pole vaulter', or 'Trying to communicate with them is like talking to a coffee cup'. These all capture the essence of the idea in – the crucial point – images that everyone immediately understands.

- *Comparisons* likewise stir our imagination. In *The Mysterious Universe*, the astronomer James Jeans captured the vastness of space by estimating that there are as many stars in the sky as there are grains of sand on all the world's beaches. Now, he may not be strictly accurate in this; indeed, one modern astronomer estimates that he is orders of magnitude in error. But that is really not the point. The sheer mind-boggling size of the number – which anyone can contemplate – gives the impression that the writer wanted to convey. Think about images appropriate to your work.

- *Metaphor* is a scientist's prime ally in the battle to explain research to a lay audience. Biologists are ahead of the game in exploiting metaphor. Cell biologists have constructed a whole drama in which proteins act as workers, supervisors and managers in the cellular factory, taking their coded instructions from head office where genes direct operations. Immunology too has a superb, overarching military metaphor: immune cells acting as a defence force against invaders. In this microscopic battleground you will even find the biochemical equivalents of uniforms, flags and communication lines. Of course, a metaphor is only a graphic approximation. It is not the real thing. Remember, when trying to devise metaphors to explain your own research, that they are to aid communication to a lay audience not to explain your work to your peers.

- *Anecdote*. Research is a human activity and, as such, will inevitably generate interesting human stories. Everyone remembers, albeit in a mutilated form, the story of Fleming's discovery of the action of penicillin on his contaminated dish. But, every day of the year in some laboratory around the world, something surprising, unexpected, foolish or dramatic happens. Serendipity plays a larger part in science than most people imagine – Pasteur, Röntgen and Becquerel were just three of its beneficiaries – and that sort of occurrence makes for good listening/viewing/reading. If you can set your research within some anecdotal framework it will help both to make it memorable and to 'humanize' you.

- *Humour* too is entertaining and useful. If your work, for all its ultimate seriousness, has an amusing element in it, exploit that in your media interaction. During the Summer of the year 2000, the joint European Space Agency/NASA mission to Saturn, the Cassini-Huygens space probe, was making its way to its distant planetary target. It occurred to one of the mission scientists, John Zarnecki of the University of Kent, that, as the probe swung by the Earth, it would slow its orbital motion by a vanishingly small amount – one million millionth of a second. On the face of it, this is not particularly remarkable. Even so, the whole Cassini-Huygens mission was able to command a lot of attention when Professor Zarnecki pointed out that this meant, in effect, that the much-anticipated celebrations for the new millennnim would be delayed! This made a catchy headline (in the vein of 'Hold the champagne') and also illustrated the value of coupling research stories to some current event of general interest. Astronomers over the years have done something similar towards the end of December by finding candidate stars or supernovae to explain the biblical Star of Bethlehem.

Pictures, then, are valuable to you in interviews. So too is a certain amount of reflexivity. Bring yourself and your feelings into the interview if appropriate. When discussing potentially dangerous environmental hazards, for example, it strengthens your case if you say things like: 'I have a family/partner/friends too and I'm worried about it', or, 'You've every right to ask that question. I would too in your place,' and so on. In other words, be yourself.

Can things go wrong?

Let us return finally to Dr X. Her case is not wholly fanciful, but the chances of its happening are quite slim – and they can be severely reduced if one comes to the whole business of interacting with the media with a mind prepared along the lines suggested above.

On the whole, out and out misrepresentation is rare. Journalists like to get their stories accurate and fair. It would be quite foolhardy for a reporter to incur the wrath and suspicion of key organizations such as colleges, universities and other institutions which represent a constant source of stories. So symbiosis rather than parasitism is the relationship you should expect. Both sides should benefit from the interaction.

Editors' note ∎

There are a number of agencies throughout the world which exist to support the efforts of higher education and research institutes to popularize their work. Among those available to UK institutions are Universities UK (formerly the Committee of Vice-Chancellors and Principals) and AlphaGalileo.

Universities UK works with a global Internet-based expert search service for journalists called ProfNet. This enables press offices to receive daily email which list enquiries from journalists in search of specific academic experts. You can find out more about the service via the website www.profnet.com

Universities UK also works to promote university activities in the national media and hosts regular events for university press officers. Further information from www.universitiesuk.ac.uk

AlphaGalileo is a free service funded by the British, French and German governments, the Wellcome Trust and some of the British research councils. It exists to make European science and technology news available to the world's media. AlphaGalileo uses the Internet to provide press releases, a calendar of events and an address book of European science public relations staff. Users must register via the electronic form at www.alphagalileo.org Those who work in science public relations and register as a contributor are able to put news and event information on to the site. Journalists see embargoed news items and have the opportunity to receive email alerts of new items likely to be of interest to them.

By the beginning of summer 2000, over 1800 journalists had registered and almost 900 contributors. They are able to see over 3500 releases covering all aspects of science and technology from archaeology to medicine and computers to the environment. Further information from www.alphagalileo.org or email site.editor@alphagalileo.org

Further reading ∎

Albrighton, F. (2001) *Can I Quote You on That?*, 2nd edn. Manchester: Association of University Administrators.

White, S., Evans, P., Mihill, C. and Tysoe, M. (1993) *Hitting the Headlines*. Leicester: British Psychological Society.

8

WHY AREN'T WE SPEAKING TO EACH OTHER?
Internal communications

**Frank Albrighton and
Julia Thomas**

How many times have you heard it said when something goes wrong in an organization that it was a 'breakdown in communications'? Very often this is the easy way out because it blames the *process* of communication for a fault rather than those who are charged with communicating. Communication is very much like driving a car: it is something which we do well but everyone else does very badly.

All agree that communications, and internal communications in particular, are important in an institution. Higher education institutions have a tradition of sharing knowledge and of collegiality: a culture which should facilitate the easy exchange of information amongst members of a scholarly community. Perhaps because of this tradition, internal communications in higher education institutions often do not get much further than being recognized as a good thing. Good practice is some way behind. In the so-called real world of industry and commerce, failures of internal communication can have spectacularly serious results in failures of performance and, at worse, strikes. Consequently, captains of industry take this matter seriously. In a survey in February 2000, one hundred of Britain's leading board directors were asked which people matter to them.[1] They were asked: 'In order to achieve business success, how important do you feel it is for a major company to work on developing goodwill with the following groups?' The results are illustrated in Figure 8.1.

If these results are transferable to a higher education context – and since they concern human relationships rather than products or services, they perhaps can be – this is very sobering news for an external relations department. If we say that existing customers equate to students and that employees are the same in both cases, then the chart suggests that a far greater proportion of our efforts should be devoted to our internal audiences. It is interesting that some of those audiences that we worry about most – local community, local government, the media – are judged by these business leaders as being the least important in terms of the success of their activities. The high importance given to communications with employees is based on three assertions. First, staff who are well informed are more likely to be involved in the aims of the institution. Second, staff who are involved are more likely to perform effectively. Third, it is the duty of management to inform staff about what is going on in their organization. These are worthy and laudable sentiments, but how effectively are they translated into practice? Let us look again at the private sector.

In 1998, the Marketing and Communication Agency undertook the first survey of its kind to assess the level of commitment by employees to the success of their organization.[2] The results showed that the majority of employees in Britain's biggest organizations feel undervalued, uninvolved and lack confidence in their leaders' organization and vision. Only 9 per cent of employees surveyed thought that their views and participation were valued by their organization. Only 15 per cent had confidence in their leaders and only 16 per cent believed in their organization's vision for the future. The study also showed that low levels of commitment and understanding are endemic across all levels of staff: managers are only slightly more committed than non-managers to their company's goals and show no more understanding of the overall goals than their staff.

Another survey at about the same time found that only 11 per cent of all workers in the UK strongly agree with the statement: 'I trust and believe what the directors of my company say.'[3]

What does this mean for higher education? Two things at least. The first is that if we believe that we have lessons to learn from the world of business then we should take very seriously our internal communications. The second is that even though the leaders of industry regard employees as hugely important to their business' success, they have not managed to involve them in or motivate them towards acting for the success of the company. So you might say there actually is nothing to be learned from the private sector

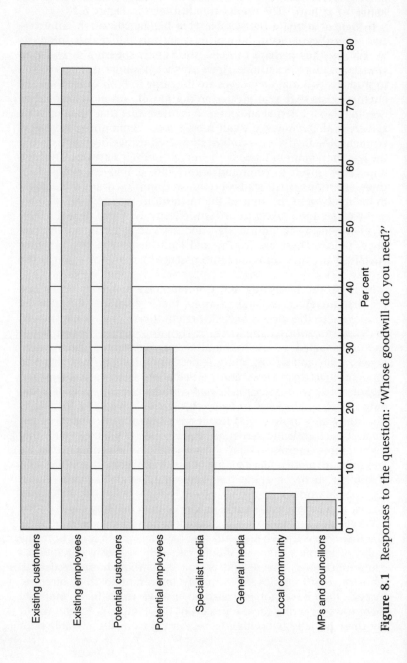

Figure 8.1 Responses to the question: 'Whose goodwill do you need?'

and our traditional informal methods of communication work much better, or at least no worse.

In spite of all the survey data we have quoted above, the effectiveness of communications is a notoriously difficult area to measure. In the early 1990s, in the University of Birmingham we wanted to stimulate a debate on this subject and undertook some informal and probably unrepresentative research to try to spark off a discussion. Taking a lead from the way our friends in the media sample public opinion, we took a video camera out on to campus and stopped members of the university to question them. The first question we put to them was: 'How many students do you think there are in the university?' Bearing in mind that this is a piece of information that appears in practically every publication the university produces, and is repeated frequently in internal newsletters and other communications, the answers we were given varied enormously. The lowest was 1000, which would have meant that our big civic University actually had fewer students than the school next door. And the largest was a breathtaking 100,000. You could argue that, for many people in the university, this is not a piece of information that has immediate impact on their daily lives or the way they go about their business, but it is such a fundamental fact that we thought that, one way or another, we ought to have communicated it. This gave us little confidence that we had communicated anything at all about the conduct of university business and decision-making. The obvious conclusion is that although the university has been busy publishing information repeatedly, very little of it has sunk in at the receiving end. This is a failure of management, not a fault of the employee. It is too easy at the centre of an organization involved daily in corporate matters to believe that making information available is the same as communicating. Perhaps we are no better than industry after all.

Our second question on this vox pop exercise was designed to see whether members of the university had a shared perception of the organization they worked for. We did this by the device of saying to people: 'If the university were a car, what kind of a car would it be?' Some staff deserve credit for supreme loyalty by likening the University of Birmingham to a Rolls-Royce or a Jaguar (which was at the time regarded as the correct answer). Others were a bit more challenging with middle-of-the-range models like a Ford Sierra and a Vauxhall Cavalier. In the minds of some staff, their employer was a Citroën 2CV or 'one of those old American models with chromium fins on'.

This is the real world in which mission statements, corporate messages and integrated marketing strategies have to make their mark. Evidence from a number of universities, some researched and some anecdotal, reveals a number of common themes about internal communications. One is a lack of understanding between people at the centre of the institution and those who are working in academic departments. There is a general perception that the central management makes demands without a full understanding of how life is 'at the coal-face'.

Another general concern in several universities and in other organizations is that, however good the communication from the management to the staff, mechanisms for upward communications are not very effective. A junior member of staff who has a useful point to contribute finds that they have to make a great effort to ensure that it is heard by those in power. If their comment can be perceived as being critical of management decisions, there is always a certain hesitation at being too prominent a critic. As higher education institutions generally become managerial in their style, there is a widespread feeling that what the media call 'ordinary people' cannot influence decisions before they are made and then it is too late afterwards.

The principal means of internal communication in print at the University of Birmingham is the internal 'Bulletin', the close counterpart of many similar internal newsletters in other institutions. In a recent readership survey we tried to find out how the 'Bulletin' compared with other sources of information about the university. One of the questions we asked was: 'Where do you get information about the university?' What respondents said is shown graphically in Figure 8.2.

We were surprised to see that 60 per cent mentioned circulars and memoranda as a source of information. It seemed high, but perhaps is symptomatic of an academic environment where people think of written communication as the most effective and durable way of talking to each other and recording their communication. The 'Bulletin' came out at 55 per cent, which was in line with national statistics for similar-sized organizations. Particularly interesting was the fact that the grapevine scored at 48 per cent as a source of information for employees of the university about their employer and its activities. This is a very uncomfortable figure.

The next question we asked was: 'Where would you *prefer* to get information about the university?' The results are shown in Figure 8.3.

Circulars and memos still score very highly and the 'Bulletin' is pretty much the same. The most spectacular fall is in the grapevine. This seems to say that, however much people delight in gossip and rumour they would really rather not rely on them as sources of information about their work.

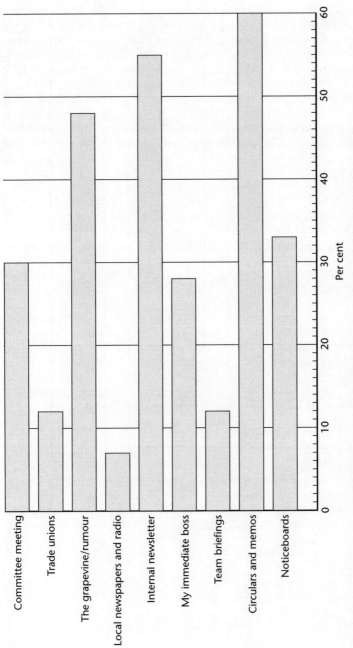

Figure 8.2 Responses to the question: 'Where do you get information about the university?'

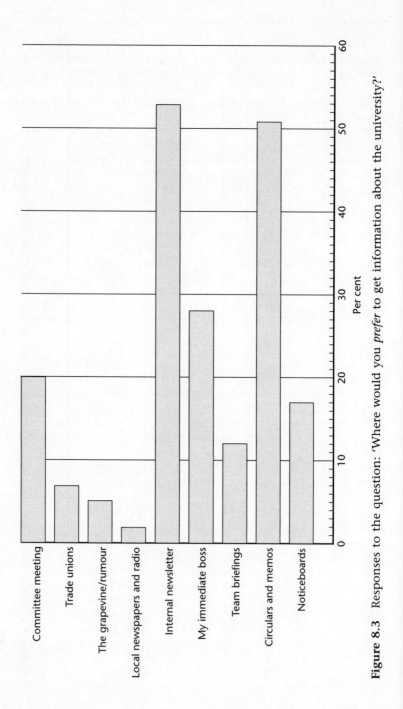

Figure 8.3 Responses to the question: 'Where would you *prefer* to get information about the university?'

There are three methods of communication which involve conversations between managers and employees. If the categories immediate boss, team briefings and meetings are considered together and regarded simply as 'talking to each other', then this is also scoring highly. The simple conclusion from this study is that people would like to learn about their environment in writing and in meetings, particularly those addressed by their immediate boss.

The printed word is a very effective means of communication. The writer can prepare words which are carefully dedicated to their purpose. The reader can absorb the words and reconsider them in order to understand fully their meaning. Most internal newsletters in higher education institutions are largely indistinguishable from each other. We are not alone in this. Commercial organizations also publish house magazines. These magazines contain good news about the company which is very much passed down from the top to the workers. They tell employees what is going on without taking them into the confidence of the management. As in education, they do not encourage debate. Even where there is a letters or opinion column available to readers it is rare for there to be a serious discussion of policy matters. The outstanding exception, of course, is matters to do with car parking. It is well known in higher education management circles throughout the country that if you want to divert attention from some controversial decision, the thing to do is increase the car parking charges.

One problem with printed publications is that they have to reach such a wide spread of readers if they are to be successful. The outcome in the majority of higher education institutions is a newsletter which reflects the preoccupations and interest of the management. It is therefore addressed principally to academic staff and administrative staff, rarely relating directly to the interests of others, except sometimes through personalia or parish magazine news which can all too easily become patronizing.

Another problem with written communications – for the management and for the external relations officer – is that if you try genuinely to report what is going on then you should publish the bad news as well as the good. If you do this then it will be picked by the real media who can then blow it up into something out of all proportion. How can you discuss matters openly in the institution, airing your problems without damaging your reputation externally?

Some major companies use video to communicate with their employees. This is a very powerful medium and one that can be controlled to the extent even of its being manipulative. But whereas in a company it is possible to require staff to be in a particular place at a particular time to watch the video, this could not realistically be achieved in higher education institutions.

The most effective means of communication is one person talking to another, and we saw that employees welcome meetings and conversations, especially with their immediate superiors. A good departmental manager will have in place internal structures that ensure that departmental business is discussed and shared as much and as quickly as possible. Within the small unit of a department it is possible to respond to comments and questions in an informal, family atmosphere that is much more difficult to achieve across a whole institution. Even at departmental level, however, the communication has to be positive and sustained by the manager. The departmental head who says, 'My door is always open', or 'Just tell me what you want to know and I'll brief you', is not really doing anything at all to communicate effectively.

What about committees? They traditionally have been the way in which members of staff (by which we have really meant the academic staff) have been represented in institutional management, from the departmental committee to the governing body itself. Memberships are carefully planned so as to have a balanced, representative membership, and in some cases elections are held to ensure popular support. Unfortunately, this does not work. Only rarely will members carefully sound out their constituencies before attending a meeting so that they are at least informed of the views of others. Even less common is a systematic reporting back so that information and decisions are widely disseminated throughout the community. In most institutions the number of committees has been drastically reduced in recent years, concentrating power in relatively few bodies attended by senior managers and lay members. Only senates remain as places where, from time to time, an issue can be of sufficient controversy to arouse widespread concern and a vehement expression of popular opinion. As a regular means of communication within the institution, committees are not the answer.

Is there no way in which the effectiveness of face-to-face meetings can be harnessed to aid internal communications? For many companies the answer is a system of team briefings – a method advocated by the Industrial Society. Team briefings work as follows. Every month after the board of directors meets, the three or four key decisions that have to be communicated to the workforce are identified. Those key decisions then constitute the core messages which are passed on to the next layer of management below the board in a team briefing session. The team briefer presents the core messages and adds any local messages which are relevant to the members of the group. The members of that group then become team briefers themselves and address further groups, and so on down the organization. The local messages are not cumulative but are devised as being appropriate for each level.

To implement this procedure properly there are some rules that have to be followed. For example, in industry, where time means money in a rather more direct way than in higher education, meetings have to be short – no more than thirty minutes because, while the meeting is going on, productivity is halted. In some companies a system has been adopted where the factory stops while the workforce is being briefed.

The next important point is that the overall process has to be rapid, taking no more than 48 hours from the meeting of the board until everyone has been reached. Already you will have identified reasons why it would be difficult to introduce a system like this in an uncompromising manner in higher education.

There is another reason that probably makes team briefing in higher education institutions even more unlikely. An important part of the Industrial Society team briefing process is an understanding that a question asked in a briefing by an employee will always be answered either by the team leader there and then or by a more senior person within 48 hours. From the meeting of the board of directors it takes 48 hours for the messages to find their way to every employee of the workforce, and within a further 48 hours every question emanating from any employee about these issues will have been answered.

Team briefings are a method of communication being taken seriously by many major organizations in this country at present. This is not lip service to keeping employees informed but without involving them in the difficult issues. It is a serious attempt to share with them the issues that are preoccupying management and to attempt to answer their questions about what is involved. It treats employees as partners in the enterprise. It also helps to ensure that managers give the right messages to the right people.

Our purpose in describing this process in detail is to make the point that to tackle internal communications radically involves a disciplined and committed approach by management. You really must mean to do it and be prepared not only to put time into the process but also to discuss issues openly, even when they are hard questions. Ask yourself: are you prepared to do that?

If what we are saying is that conventional methods of internal communications are either ineffectual or too daunting to be achievable in the peculiar atmosphere of higher education, is there then any hope for an effective communications mechanism? If the answer lies anywhere, it is probably in the World Wide Web. The web has a number of characteristics that distinguish it from other methods of communication. Production processes are virtually eliminated. There is no time lapse between a decision by management to say something and the opportunity for employees to read it. It can be updated rapidly. Matters can be discussed as they develop, without management's having to make difficult decisions on when the time is right. It bypasses committees and hierarchical management structures and enables those at the top or centre of the institution – whichever image you prefer – to communicate directly with all individual employees.

There is a practical problem here, however, in that although there is general web access for academic, administrative and secretarial staff in most institutions, there are large numbers of employees whose duties, because they are not office-based or because they are part-time, do not allow them ready access to the web.

Most important of all, the web makes it genuinely possible to encourage interaction and discussion. By the simple inclusion of an email address, management can encourage comment, question and can decide whether this is a one-to-one correspondence or a more public debate by means of a bulletin board. Judgements such as this can be made in the light of particular circumstances and issues.

But if the web solves the problems surrounding which medium to use, it still leaves the political and policy issues as difficult as ever to solve. If the web makes it possible for management easily and quickly to share decisions and preoccupations with employees, then what reason does it have for not doing so? If the web makes it possible for employees quickly and easily to raise questions and make comments, what reason does management have for not listening? The web makes internal communications possible in a unique way. It isolates the difficult issues to do with control, power and secrecy that are the real root of internal communications problems. Higher education institutions that say they are dedicated to open government and debate will increasingly find themselves challenged to put these principles into effect.

Notes

1 *The Importance of Stakeholder Relationships to Business Success* (2000). London: MORI.
2 *The Buy-in Benchmark: A Survey of Staff Understanding and Commitment and the Impact on Business Performance* (1998). London: Marketing and Communication Agency.
3 *Workers' Attitudes to Bosses* (1998). London: Smythe Dorward Lambert.

9

GUESS WHO'S COMING TO DINNER!
Event management

Frank Albrighton and Julia Thomas

Event management is the Cinderella of external relations. Too often it is seen merely as a mechanical process concerned with tedious details like booking coaches and making sure that the coffee turns up on time. This is pretty dreary stuff, compared with arranging television interviews, directing photo shoots or publishing glossy brochures. But that attitude is wrong. Events in many ways should be seen as the centrepiece of what an institution can do to influence its different audiences.

One of the most powerful ways of influencing someone's opinion, short of actually brainwashing them, is to meet in circumstances which you control, treat them generously and courteously, and then talk to them. The biggest deals are clinched in one-to-one meetings or at small dinner parties. Secret diplomacy depends on the subtlety and sophistication of dialogue. Mass communication techniques are important in external relations but we use them because we have to, because we cannot possibly talk to every one of our constituencies on an individual basis. The great virtue of events is that they can go some way towards simulating this face-to-face contact. They are almost always, for example, occasions on which representatives of your institution meet, either individually or in a group, members of your target audiences. They are most often occasions on your own premises where you can present what you do and where you do it in the best possible light. Events provide an opportunity for you to make powerful impressions on some of your most important constituencies. You will miss the point if you regard them as tedious exercises, and you will miss some important opportunities.

One of the reasons for the low reputation of event management is that we tend to think of large-scale events – seminars, conferences, open days and so on – where we are inevitably preoccupied with making things work well and it is easy to become distracted from the main purpose. But events are much more than this. In the context of external relations, *all* encounters have a communications perspective. This means that event management in its broadest sense encompasses everything from small dinner parties and select receptions in the principal's residence to visits by royalty, open days, alumni reunions, public meetings, donor cultivation occasions, press conferences, launches of new initiatives and openings of new buildings. The list goes on: public lectures, graduation ceremonies, visits by research sponsors, audits of one kind or another are all opportunities that can be exploited to enhance the reputation and the positioning of an institution.

It is as important in event management as in any other area of external relations to be absolutely clear about why you are doing what you are doing and what you hope to achieve from it. There are two aspects to this. The first arises from those events and occasions that are a regular part of any institution's calendar. We all have award ceremonies; we all have cultural events like lectures and concerts. We all have a pattern of hospitality by the most senior members of the institution that has probably developed over many years, loosely related to policy issues and influenced by the personal inclination of those offering hospitality to the institution's guests. It is likely, however, that what happens at these occasions and who is invited has not been subjected to an objective and rigorous analysis of its usefulness and productivity for the institution. To do that may appear to be trespassing in areas of the personal social life of senior people, but if the events and social occasions are held in the name of (and paid for by) the institution then it is legitimate to review their nature, purpose and effectiveness to see what benefits the institution is gaining.

It is easy to make ready assumptions about why such events happen and what benefits they give. It is important, however, to challenge them with some of the most basic questions. Whom is this occasion for? What message are we trying to convey to them? How will the form of the event – the people they meet and the arrangements – generally help to convey that message? How will we prevent occasions from degenerating into parties for ourselves at which the majority of the guests are members of the institution talking to each other?

It so happens that as we write this chapter the University of Birmingham is in the midst of its centenary year 2000. When we observed – from a distance – that the centenary of the award of the university's charter coincided with the new millennium, we decided that the centenary of a provincial redbrick university would pale into insignificance alongside what we expected to be the spectacular year-long worldwide party for the new millennium. As it turned out, the millennium never really happened on that scale. However, we did think that the millennium would make more impact than it did and concluded that our celebrations should be spread over a twelve-month period, being little more than an enhancement of our normal university events. In a climate of financial prudence we thought we should not splash out on a big celebration and that only modest contributions of money and time would enable us to mark the centenary appropriately but not extravagantly.

This was the view from two years in advance; but as the centenary year approached, the institution's expectations grew and many people saw interesting and imaginative ways in which they could exploit the occasion – not just to have a good time, but also to support their core activities. This meant that centenary events grew both in number and in the scale of their ambition.

The outcome is that the university's celebrations included two royal visits, two concerts in Birmingham's Symphony Hall, a lecture in the Birmingham Repertory Theatre, a service in Birmingham Cathedral, a gala dinner with Jools Holland and his Rhythm and Blues Orchestra, an open air Funday with Bjorn Again and Roy Wood, an all-night student party in the centre of the campus, the unveiling of two works of art, an exhibition, a high profile event in Chicago, twenty alumni reunions on the campus and other reunions in nine countries in Europe, North America and the Far East. (And those were only the events. We also published an official history, sold a range of gifts and souvenirs and ran a £1.3 million centenary fund-raising campaign.) Without a robust organization and an adequate budget to support the events we could not have coped with the incessant demands of arranging all these events. We could also have used a large dose of prescience.

If you have many events to arrange, as we did, or if you have a very large or important occasion like an open day, a fair or a royal visit, it is quite likely that you will need additional staff resources. You may decide to hire someone onto the staff, or you may prefer to engage an outside agency. It will relieve a lot of the pressure if you have outside help, but make sure that your contractors understand and are sensitive to your institution's style and culture. Experience of running a pop festival or the launch of a new car may not translate very well to your event.

If you do involve extra people – inside or outside – those people will still need to be managed; and if you want to avoid doing the job yourself, their knowledge and relevant experience will make all the difference.

Whatever the scale of the occasion, whether it is an intimate private dinner party or a public open day involving tens of thousands of visitors, there are a number of elements that are crucial to achieving a successful outcome.

Everything begins with a plan. You must always have a plan that takes account of *every* detail. Whatever the occasion it is well worth working through it almost minute by minute to ensure that you have thought of everything. Your self-examination should begin something like this:

- Does it matter what route they follow to the campus?
- Which gate will they enter by?
- Where will they park their cars?
- How shall we get them from the car park to the building?
- What if it's raining?
- Who will receive them at the building?
- Do we need any signs?
- Are there security issues – for cars, for coats, for people?
- What do we do about people who arrive early?
- When do we start to serve the drinks?
- What about special dietary requirements?
- When are the speeches?
- Do we need a public address system?
- Who will tell them it is time to sit down for dinner?

The list goes on, but unless you subject your plans to this amount of detailed examination you run the risk that the event will go wrong because of some small, unforeseen eventuality. You cannot over-plan an important event.

The best laid plans are vulnerable to human intervention. The next principle is that everyone must be briefed. Again, you must think about every individual, from the security officer on the gate to the head of the institution. We have heard reports of someone who was turned away from an institution by the security staff, being told, 'You can't go in there, there is an important event on'. Little did that officer know that he was addressing the guest of honour himself. At another institution the principal was not aware that everyone else was assuming that he would entertain one of the guests during an interval in the proceedings. The result was that the principal went off to make some telephone calls and the VIP guest was left looking forlornly for someone to talk to.

The briefing should include not only those who have a major role to perform but also those members of the institution who are included to mix with the guests. It seems obvious, but they do need to be told what the occasion is, who the guests are and why they themselves are present. This last part should include telling them to talk to the visitors and not get into a huddle with their cronies, gossiping about university politics.

The next rule is: Assume Nothing. You cannot assume that the main gate will be open on your day of days just because it has been open every day for the past fifty years. You cannot assume the contractors will not arrive to dig up the main drive. You cannot assume that this is not the annual catering staff holiday. You cannot assume that because a head of department has agreed that you may bring a visitor to the laboratories that these will be presentable with articulate people on hand to explain the work. As you go through the line-by-line planning process, you should check everything, challenge everything and satisfy yourself at least once that everything that is planned will actually happen.

The next principle may seem slightly out of place in a higher education environment. It is that you should not be afraid to go a little bit over the top. So much of what we do has to be restrained, sober, understated and subtle that it is possible to misjudge events by not adding the touch of flamboyance that can make all the difference. Music always helps. What about engaging students at your event to provide a little chamber music or some gentle jazz? If you want a party atmosphere you ought to have champagne or at least sparkling wine. The presence of a showbusiness personality – ideally an alumnus – will transform the number of acceptances that you receive for your event. In this context a household name really does have to mean what it says. The chairman of the foundation, the chief executive of the company or the leading politician may all be very important contacts and important in their own field but they will never have the pulling power of someone 'as seen on TV'. Event management is the second cousin of show business and you can let yourself go a bit.

Whether you are organizing a major multifaceted event or a small occasion, you must have absolute clarity about who is responsible for what and who has authority. So much of event planning involves a number of fine judgements about what will be appropriate and what will not. One individual has to carry that final authority so that, even if they make one or two errors, there will be a consistency of style and approach through the event that will aid its integrity. This is not to say that you should not adopt a team approach in managing major occasions. It is essential to involve all the people that can affect its satisfactory progress, but at the same time there must be a clearly identified event manager who has the remit and the authority to make the event happen.

The next rule is: make sure you have enough money. How much is enough? More than you think, or, at least, more than you think when you start to plan. As your plans develop you are certain to think of new ideas, to find costs you had overlooked and to discover ways in which money can oil the wheels. In the world of devolved budgets there is a familiar sequence in which a department enthusiastically agrees to contribute to your occasion but finds that it cannot afford to do so. A sweetener will help, even if it is only to ensure that your high standards are maintained.

Whenever you can, base your budget on real estimates. You may be surprised by what it actually costs to have drinks served to 100 people, or to have a coach on standby for a day, or to hire an LCD projector and screen. These costs rapidly add up to what can be a frightening total. If it is too frightening, your event may not be worth the cost.

For some occasions it may be appropriate to charge guests. Perhaps for an alumni reunion or for a high quality entertainment. This brings a whole new set of issues to do with selling tickets, taking bookings, handling cash, insurance, reserving seats, dealing with dissatisfied customers. Proceed with great care.

Finally in this list of precepts, do not forget to review the event when it is all over. It may be necessary to follow up contacts made with individuals, to say thank you to those who contributed to the occasion, and it is important to go back to your original statement of objectives and to make a judgement, ideally a measurement, of whether you succeeded.

Although all events have certain common themes and requirements, there are some that give rise to very special considerations. Foremost among these is the royal visit. By its very nature you will want a royal occasion to be particularly successful and you will be even more rigorous and meticulous in your planning. There are, however, a number of external constraints that will affect the way you go about this. The first is involvement with the Lord Lieutenant's Office. Any visit by a member of the Royal Family will be coordinated through your county's Lord Lieutenant's Office, although the degree of detailed involvement will vary depending to the individual concerned. Different members of the Royal Family have different styles, different degrees of formality and attract different degrees of security. A visit from the Queen is in a league of its own. Similarly, the involvement of the police will have a bearing on your arrangements and may bring some disruption to normal institutional life. This can happen, for example, if a building has been inspected by the police and has to remain sealed until after the royal occasion.

The personal office of the member of the Royal Family concerned will also want to know exactly what you are planning and may well specify a number of do's and don'ts. All these requirements will be made plain to you but they can affect your plans quite fundamentally and the sooner you can learn about them the better. Having said that, it is not the custom of members of the Royal Family to agree to make visits more than a few months in advance, and to that degree your planning has to be fairly condensed.

You can expect a visit by a member of the Royal Family to attract media attention. Again, depending on who it is, the arrangements may be fairly relaxed, but for the more senior figures there may be a press rota system where only accredited journalists may attend, and they share pictures and words with other media outlets.

Members of the Royal Family will be aware that you want photographs of their visit, but their aides will protect them from being harassed; and royal visitors will never pose.

Very large public occasions also bring special requirements. Again the police will be involved if you are going to generate a great deal of traffic. There may be a need to involve the local authority for matters of health and safety, and if you plan to make a loud noise with music in the open air, for example, then there will be stringent environmental requirements you have to observe.

Organizing events in other countries – alumni reunions, for example – puts a particular strain on your planning expertise. There are the obvious difficulties of time differences and currency conversions but you must also be sensitive to cultural matters. Some of these are apparently trivial, like being aware of the time at which people would customarily expect to gather for early evening drinks or a buffet dinner. Some are much more important, as in Muslim countries, for example, where you must be sensitive to times of prayer. There is a multiplicity of issues. What is meant locally by words like 'buffet', 'reception', 'dinner'? What is the convention on dress? Will people know what you mean when you say 'black tie' or 'lounge suit'? If it is an alumni event then the best possible source of information will be one of your own alumni locally who can give sympathetic and understanding advice.

Events involving VIPs are often part of a cultivation process. This may be an element in your fundraising activities or simply a wish to become closer to people of power and influence. For such individuals it is well worth having a long-term plan. This involves knowing who you want to cultivate and managing the process of their involvement in the institution. There are obvious courtesies you must observe. For example, if you were told on the first occasion that a particular individual does not eat meat, then remember that for every subsequent occasion. (You may think of recording such information on a database, but remember that, in the UK at least, the requirements of the Data Protection Act are very strict.)

One way to structure your relationships with such VIPs is to review the whole of the year's events, both planned and possible. If your institution has, for example, a couple of prestigious lectures, some concerts, the award ceremonies, and so on, it is a good idea to list them and to think which individuals you will invite to which occasion. Themes can be useful: a concert provides a good opportunity to involve yourselves with the local arts community, for example. A lecture might be an appropriate occasion to which to invite contacts in the legal profession. One important advantage of this systematic approach is that it avoids a situation in which an important contact is encountered in some way, invited to the institution, wined, dined and feted, and then promptly forgotten. In a large organization where everyone assumes that everyone else is doing something, this is all too easy.

Events are all about people and therefore bring their own set of sensitivities and political difficulties. A few of them are discussed next.

Very senior members of the institutions are involved in the event, and upward management is not the easiest of tasks. Sometimes an event is the bright idea of the head of institution or someone very close to them. The idea is passed on for implementation with 'The principal thinks it would be good public relations if . . .' From that moment on it is a case of no questions asked. The costs may rocket, the main guests may decline your invitation and the original benefits – never tested – may be disappearing fast. We cannot tell you how to deal with this, but you should be aware of it.

'Are wives invited? Sorry, I mean spouses . . . er, no, I mean partners?' This is another tricky area. Political correctness brings enough difficulties, but what about the principle? There is a convention in some institutions that partners are included in social events. This is not necessarily the convention in other worlds – industry, for example – and we have all seen the hapless wife loyally supporting her husband at an academic dinner without wanting to be there at all. If the purpose of the occasion is to talk serious business, having partners present changes its character into a purely social event, even at the level of a seating plan that positions your chief executive next to, not the prime target, but their partner.

More mundanely, including partners doubles the cost. Will their presence double the value? Or are you really using the event as some kind of reward or acknowledgement for your own staff? You need to be clear. It may not be significant for a very occasional dinner, but for a spouse who dines regularly or travels with their partner, there may be tax implications for these benefits.

Other aspects of the culture of the academic world may need your attention. For example, we are generally fairly informal, whereas events by their nature require some structure and presentation. How do you tell the professor that, for just this once, he ought to change that well-worn jacket? Similarly, academic institutions are places of critical inquiry, but it does not do to subject your guest to a sustained assault about all that is wrong with government, industry, the schools or wherever it is they come from.

In the midst of all these sensitivities you still must devise some way of measuring the effectiveness of your event. This is even more difficult than in other areas of external relations. There are some objective measures: how many people came; whether the follow-up action was effective; whether there was any unprompted further contact by your guests. Beyond that, your judgements are likely to be fairly subjective. This is difficult because everyone involved will want the occasion to have been a success, and the fact that everyone enjoyed it is not necessarily enough. Leave it for while, stand back, and make a cool assessment of how your institution has *really* benefited from what happened.

Although we began by stressing that event management has an important strategic role to play in external relations, attention to detail is an essential prerequisite. Below is a checklist of some of the points that you ought to think about in planning events. This does not claim to be exhaustive, and not every point will be appropriate for every occasion, but it may be helpful in prompting some thoughts.

- *What is the purpose of this occasion?*
- *Who are the targets?*
- *What do you want to say to them?*
- *Date and time?* Take account of other activities in your institution – examinations and so on – and of big public events that may attract your guests. If yours is a public occasion, spread the word as widely as you can.

- *Who is going to run it?* Be clear about organizational responsibility: whether it is one person or a team. If it is a team, be very clear about who is responsible for what.
- *Badging of the event.* As well as all the detailed practical arrangements, think about having a theme for the occasion.
- *Planning.* Look at every detail of the arrangements from the point of view of the visitor. What would *you* think if we did that to you?
- *Look good.* Make sure that display materials, exhibition boards provided by departments are of the highest quality and say to your visitors, 'You're special. We have prepared for your visit.'
- *Team spirit.* Manage your team so that not only do they deliver what they say they will do, but that they turn up on time, they stay the course and they remain courteous and friendly throughout.
- *Publicity.* For a public event, choose the most effective form of publicity. It may be newspapers, it may be letters of invitation, it could even be television advertising, but make sure you achieve value for money. And do not forget to try for coverage of the event itself.
- *Travel arrangements.* Car parks, coach parks, traffic signs.
- *Signs.* To where the event is happening, for people in wheelchairs, for toilets, for refreshments.
- *Food and drink.* This is the whole purpose of the occasion at a dinner party, but equally important at a large event as people become tired and need refreshment.
- *Students.* Students make very good helpers at open days and other events where visitors may need information and guidance. Discipline is important and this is best achieved through a formal contract based on hire and reward.
- *Problems.* Emergency arrangements, first aid, lost children.

Reviewing a list that includes toilets, traffic and lost children may have persuaded you that, whatever we say, event management really is the grubby end of the business. There are innumerable nuts and bolts, it is true, but the possible strategic benefits are substantial and you will achieve great personal satisfaction when a plan comes together.

Further reading

Albrighton, F. (1989) *Open Daze*. Manchester: Association of University Administrators.

10

WHAT ARE FRIENDS FOR?
Alumni relations

Reggie Simpson

When I tell people that I am head of Alumni Relations at the London School of Economics and Political Science (LSE), I usually get one of two responses: 'What's an alumni?' or, 'Oh, you ask people for money!'

The first is quite easily explained: The word 'alumni' has its roots in the latin 'alumnus', meaning former pupil or student; 'alumni' is the plural usage. The second elicits a more detailed response: 'No, I personally don't ask alumni for money, but the work I do – keeping in touch with alumni and engaging their continued interest in the school – helps to support LSE's development efforts, of which seeking funds from alumni is a key strategy. However, this is not, and should not be, the only reason for keeping alumni connected to the institution. Alumni can contribute time, talent and expertise, which should be valued in equal measure to their ability to give financially . . .'

Converting the layperson is less important to me than convincing higher education colleagues to adopt this same attitude at their institutions. Even better when the vice-chancellor or head of the institution sets the example:

The cultivation of alumni is crucial for every university today. Alumni should always regard themselves as part of the wider community which the university represents. Such connections have many mutual benefits. Alumni are able to keep in touch with the academic world and attend events at their university, while the university can acquire both moral and often financial support from those who have studied there.

(Professor Anthony Giddens, LSE Director)

Building a strong alumni programme should be at the heart of every institution's external relations for the following reasons:

- Alumni, better than most, understand and can represent the educational mission, needs and goals of the institution.
- Alumni have a vested interest in ensuring that the value – to themselves and to future generations of students – of the higher education they received is not diminished.
- Alumni are an important part of the institution's marketing mix. They comprise a growing external constituency, already favourably disposed towards the institution and which, through use of sophisticated data collection and maintenance, can be easily targeted and mobilized.

As Professor Giddens says, an institution and its alumni should serve each other for mutual gain. For LSE, this is embodied in the Alumni Relations mission statement:

To initiate, develop and nurture a *lifelong* relationship with alumni – underpinned by a sustained level of activity, communication, service and 'customer care' – so as to interest and engage them in active, meaningful and ongoing support of the institution's strategic objectives.

Such areas of contribution include:

- careers advice, mentoring and jobs placements for students, alumni
- recruitment of quality students
- financial support
- enhancing the image of the institution
- advice and advocacy (campaigning)
- institutional governance
- market intelligence.

The following are some specific examples of how LSE alumni help the school:

- Before the recruiters go forth on a mission to find future LSE students, they first make contact with alumni to collect 'intelligence' on the local scene: information about the region, which courses to promote, and other factors which might influence student choice.

- Administrators, charged with the task of identifying future governors of the LSE, turn to the alumni office for help in finding alumni whose expertise or connections might be of particular value.
- Academic departments undergoing 'quality assurance audits' survey their alumni to gauge post-LSE employability and the relevance of course content to 'the real world'.
- Students making Annual Fund telephone calls to Germany will already have been briefed by the German Friends organization about the local culture of philanthropy and the most tax efficient ways of giving in Germany.
- The Press and Public Relations Office uses alumni around the world to help place press releases, monitor local press coverage for LSE mentions, and to translate articles.

You may involve alumni similarly, or in other ways; perhaps not at all. Bear in mind that LSE's alumni relations programme is well established compared with those of many British and European universities.

Organizational and budgetary considerations

It is important that Alumni Relations functions within an internal environment that allows it to grow and thrive. In the early days, Alumni Relations officers often reported to the registrar, bursar or secretary. Now, they are mainly located in development or external relations offices. LSE's alumni programme sits within the Office of Development and Alumni Relations.

Most alumni operations are wholly dependent on the institution for organizational and financial support. To help offset costs and increase alumni involvement, some alumni programmes charge annual subscriptions, offering a range of benefits and services to 'members only'. There has been a trend away from subscription-based alumni associations to those that embrace all alumni.

What is the right model for your institution? Ask yourself some key questions. What does your institution hope to accomplish with support from alumni? What can you offer alumni in return? Have you got sufficient resources? Is there commitment from the very top? When giving consideration to these matters, it is important to make clear that the alumni population is not static; it grows year on year, and therefore your revenue stream, from whatever source or sources, must be increased accordingly.

Building a programme

Alumni programmes are as diverse as the institutions they serve, but they all share the same basic components. These are discussed below.

Alumni records (database)

Establishing and maintaining a database of alumni is the most important investment you can make for your alumni programme – you cannot communicate with alumni if you have no contact details, nor invite their participation or solicit their support. Equally, you will need to ensure appropriate data management procedures: for example, have you got enough data entry staff?

Ideally, you want a flexible database system that allows you to record and extract data efficiently, and which allows you to manipulate or segment the data to best advantage. Some databases can even help you manage your events administration (ticketing, billing) and membership subscription collection and renewal. Because alumni are a major target for fundraising, the database is usually shared with development colleagues for recording donor information, generating reports and gift administration.

There are a number of alumni and fundraising software packages on the market, although some institutions have developed their own. Whether home-grown or bespoke, the alumni database should be robust enough to leave room for expansion, particularly as your alumni population is growing.

Communications

If the budget is tight and you have to restrict yourself to one activity, then keeping in touch with alumni should be your main concern. The traditional way of doing so is to produce a newsletter or magazine, filled with information about your institution which keeps alumni up to date, and news of fellow alumni. Research in the United States has confirmed that the most widely read sections of any alumni publication are the 'class notes' and the obituaries.

At LSE, it is the Press and Information Office that produces the alumni publication. The award-winning 'LSE Magazine' is distributed to all 60,000 LSE alumni twice a year, free of charge. It combines features about various LSE initiatives and academic pursuits, social commentary and other issue-focused articles, with the Office of Development and Alumni Relations providing a round-up of alumni events and activities, class notes, obituaries, and news of fundraising projects and successes.

A biannual alumni magazine cannot give instantaneous news, nor is it a particularly 'environmentally friendly' means of communication. Electronic communication, particularly through the World Wide Web, is fast becoming *the* way to communicate with alumni. A number of companies, mainly in the United States, specialize in designing bespoke alumni websites, with interactive features such as searchable email directories, chat rooms and discussion forums, online mentoring and careers schemes, classified advertisements, merchandise sales, auctions, permanent email addresses, even 'virtual events'. Many institutions now offer downloadable versions of the alumni publication.

Neither written communication nor electronic technology will ever be as effective as face-to-face communication. Nor can photos or web cameras replace a personal visit back to your campus.

Events

On-campus events provide golden opportunities to showcase your institution and how it has evolved since the alumnus left. Equally, a return to the campus, especially for those who have not returned for some time, evokes nostalgic feelings of one's student days. Reunions, which bring back groups of alumni (by year group, special interest), are particularly good vehicles for blending old and new. Reunions can be structured in many ways:

- annual reunion day or weekend for all alumni
- five year intervals: in a year ending in '0', year groups for all years ending in '0' or '5' have reunions; the following year, year groups ending in '1' and '6' hold their reunions, and so on
- anniversary year reunions: fifth, tenth, twentieth
- alumni milestone anniversary reunions: silver, golden jubilee
- special interest group reunions: department-focused, student societies or sports clubs
- special institutional milestones, for example, the centenary of the institution's founding.

You might also consider 'cluster' reunions, which bring several year-groups together at the same time. Cluster reunions may increase attendance at reunions and help to reunite those alumni who knew others in years above or below their own.

Other alumni events you might employ to bring alumni back to campus include:

- socials (dinners, receptions)
- lectures, seminars
- professional networking gatherings.

These can be organized solely by the alumni staff or be events put on by other institutional departments to which alumni can be invited (lectures, launch events).

Alumni events can also happen off campus in the neighbourhood:

- cultural/educational (museum tours, theatre visits)
- sporting events
- miscellaneous (for example, getting an MP who is an alumnus to host a reception at the House of Commons; a company tour in your institution 'catchment' area).

Much planning and preparation goes into an event. Give yourself enough time to organize one properly. Alumni, too, need enough advance notice. Above all, do not plan events in a vacuum: get feedback from alumni as to what events would most likely attract them back to campus.

Geographic alumni clubs

Alumni cannot always get back to your institution – so bring the institution to them. Most universities have distant alumni who require special efforts to keep them connected and involved. A network of geographic or regional alumni clubs can help the alumni programme reach more alumni, as well as help the institution extend its visibility and influence away from campus.

Of LSE's 60,000 alumni, more than 30,000 reside outside the UK. LSE is fortunate to have alumni clubs in 62 countries. These are largely self-supporting organizations run by committees of alumni volunteers. In countries where there are not enough alumni to merit or sustain an alumni group, there is usually an alumnus who serves as the LSE's local contact, which usually means answering questions from prospective students or fellow alumni, and generally flying the LSE flag in his or her part of the world.

The active alumni clubs put on an array of events and activities: social and cultural events, monthly meetings at a regular location, lectures, conferences, professional networking events – much the same that is provided back at the campus but in a locally flavoured format.

The visit of an academic to the country or region because of research interests or on the invitation of a third party offers one of the best and most affordable opportunities for a club to bring local alumni together. This works if: (a) the academic has the time and is willing to include meeting with alumni in his or her plans, and (b) if the alumni office or the club is given advance notice of the visit. There is nothing worse than finding out from your alumni that an academic was 'spotted' locally and no advantage for club or institution could be taken. To avoid this situation, it is best to keep track of some of the more itinerant academics, meet with them often, and impress upon them the value of including visits with alumni in their travel plans.

It is perhaps in the area of overseas student recruitment that alumni can offer their greatest contribution to the institution. Feedback to recruiters on the local 'climate' for recruitment has already been mentioned, as has fielding queries from prospective students. Alumni clubs can also help by staffing stands at recruitment fairs, visiting local feeder schools, or by hosting events to which prospective students are invited.

Alumni groups can also help to ensure that intending students have as much local support and advice before they physically appear on your campus. A pre-departure briefing or event hosted by alumni club members can go a long way in answering final questions and allaying fears.

Alumni clubs can help to smooth the transition for students returning to the locality, too. The early support efforts of an alumni club can only help to encourage younger alumni to join the club.

Special-interest clubs

General, all-inclusive alumni programmes do not work for everyone. Special-interest alumni groups cater for those alumni whose affinity to the institution is defined in more focused ways, for example by their academic department or degree programme, the student society or sporting activity they participated in, or the profession they now pursue.

At LSE, this means a special-interest group for lawyers, a media group and a group for those who are interested in the environment. Each is run by a volunteer committee and charges a membership subscription to offset costs and provide services to members, the vast majority of whom are within striking distance of the campus. Some administrative support is provided by the alumni office.

Activities which special-interest alumni groups might undertake include:

- lectures, debates, conferences
- newsletters
- professional journals

- networking
- membership directories
- fundraising for specific projects, scholarships
- mentoring of current students
- 'real world' advice and curriculum input to academic departments.

Special interest alumni groups should be encouraged to form and flourish. But, be forewarned: they can be extremely labour intensive for the alumni office, unless you can convince academic departments, the students' union or other institutional offices to share the responsibility, not just reap the rewards.

Starting an alumni club

More often than not, alumni groups owe their existence to one or more enthusiastic alumni who express the need for a club in their locality or interest area, and more importantly, offer to be the driving force behind its creation.

There are many steps to starting a club, particularly if, as is the case in many countries, there are stringent procedures for registering a club. Given the limitations of space, these can be consolidated into three key activities or considerations:

- Define your membership base and confirm the interest of other alumni by sending a letter, a questionnaire or holding an initial meeting or event, which also solicits additional support for serving on an organizing committee.
- Set up the club's organizational leadership and structure, including provisions for leadership succession, publicity, growing the membership, and liaison with the institution.
- Determine the club's objectives and draw up a plan, which should include how success can be measured and evaluated.

It is helpful if the alumni office can provide guidelines for club leaders.

Volunteers

Volunteers are the backbone of alumni clubs; without them, there is little hope of sustaining an alumni club programme. Equally, volunteers can play a significant role across external relations. The challenge is to harness their energies in a manner that will be mutually beneficial. Two points are worth making:

- Volunteer does not mean amateur.
- Volunteer management is about involving alumni, not using them.

There are a number of steps in volunteer management:

- recruitment
- training
- supervision
- recognition.

Many factors motivate volunteers: power, achievement, loyalty, recognition. Volunteers need to know that the work they do is appreciated. Recognition can be as simple as publishing the volunteer's name in the next alumni publication, or a letter of thanks from the head of the institution. Some institutions also have an awards scheme and recognition event.

At LSE, we bring alumni club leaders back to campus for a biennial leadership forum. This event combines update sessions about LSE initiatives with practical tips that will help the leaders run their clubs more effectively. Above all, the forum is about recognizing their volunteer support.

Without a doubt, volunteers can enhance the work of an alumni office and the larger external relations effort. But a cautionary note: volunteers take time and effort to train and manage.

Alumni services

The provision of services to alumni is another key component of alumni relations. Many alumni programmes offer a range of services, exclusive to their alumni, which help to build loyalty and goodwill. These include:

- merchandise: items of clothing, novelty items (mugs, pens) and other goods bearing the name or logo of the institution
- free or discounted access to institutional facilities, for example, the library, meeting rooms, gym, students' union, residence hall accommodation
- discounts at local hotels, restaurants
- help in locating a fellow former student, connecting with a former professor.

Some institutions take up ready-made, tailored schemes which require few resources and often generate considerable revenue. These include:

- affinity credit cards
- travel programmes
- phone cards

- alumni directories (book, CD-ROM)
- yearbooks
- insurance

Increasingly, alumni are asking their alma mater for help with careers and professional development. A number of institutions now offer an online careers service that allows employers to search a directory of alumni CVs. Today's emphasis on lifelong learning means an alumnus is potentially an institution's customer for life. Institutions that are developing distance learning packages should view their alumni as a captive market for short courses, executive education and higher degrees. Alumni may also be employers who are looking for bespoke courses for employees.

In deciding which services to offer alumni, it is always best to do some market research to determine what alumni want or need. Also, you should weigh carefully the implications of offering certain services, for example, insurance. How does such an activity fit with your institution's educational mission?

When does it all begin?

They say first impressions count. How connected alumni wish to be with their alma mater is shaped largely by the student experience, so it is crucial that the institution gets this right, beginning from the moment the student makes first contact with the institution, through the student days and beyond.

Alumni offices should devise and implement strategies for the early 'education' of students as future alumni, and cultivate students at the earliest opportunities. Strategies include:

- alumni staff presence at the freshers' fair or similar
- communication about the alumni network in prospectuses, student handbook, student publication
- networking events hosted by alumni for students
- mentoring schemes
- visible presence at graduation ceremonies.

The alumni office should also cultivate student societies as the seedbed of future alumni leaders. At LSE, we host an annual reception for student leaders, which has three principal aims:

- to raise the profile of Alumni Relations
- to thank student leaders for their contributions to LSE
- to encourage them to think of themselves as future alumni leaders.

Future trends and scenarios ■

What does the future hold for Alumni Relations? Here is a look into the crystal ball:

- *Size*. Alumni populations are growing at a sizeable rate. These will increase dramatically with the introduction of distance learning.
- *Youth*. Alumni populations will be getting 'younger' and more international. For example, at LSE, 65 per cent of the total alumni population of 60,000 are alumni who graduated or left LSE after 1980. Of this subset, 62 per cent live outside the UK.
- *Competition*. Institutions are competing daily for alumni time, interests, money – even loyalty to more than one alma mater.
- *Virtual institutions*. The 'e-student' will have a very different educational experience from his predecessors. Current alumni programming is aimed largely at 'traditionally' educated alumni.
- *Cradle to grave*. Future students, who are already 'shopping around' for the best education and all-round student experience, may also begin to weigh what their money can buy them in terms of aftercare – the provision of enhanced networks and services after graduation. How these networks and services are delivered in the future must be benchmarked against those offered or being considered by other institutions in the global marketplace.
- *Institutional expectations of 'delivery' of alumni programme*. Alumni offices will be under increased scrutiny and pressure to give performance measurements; for example, quality of data held on alumni (good addresses, lost alumni 'found', number of records containing employment information, and so on); participation rates of alumni in various events and activities; take-up of services; involvement; financial support.

Alumni and development ■

This chapter ends as it began, with a brief reference to fundraising. There is no denying that alumni are crucial to educational fundraising. Alumni and development professionals should work together, not at cross-purposes. This implies a solid working knowledge of, and respect for, what each is trying to achieve and valuing the results in equal measure, for the good of the institution.

MONEY, MONEY, MONEY
Managing the fundraising process

Elizabeth Smith

Can anyone raise large sums of money in the higher education sector? Is it possible to assess what can be achieved? If we opt for a fundraising campaign, how much will it cost and how should we plan to get started? As the need for additional income streams becomes more acute throughout higher education, these questions are being asked more and more frequently.

Should an institution build charitable income into its financial forecasting? A truthful answer for most in the UK today is, not yet. An institution should not enter into large financial commitments in anticipation of philanthropic contributions unless it has a history of philanthropic support from which to make predictions. There is, however, a body of experience, now established in the UK as well as in the United States, that can lead to reliable assumptions about a positive financial response to a well thought out and tested fundraising strategy.

Large sums are already being raised by British universities; Oxford and Cambridge led the way, but others have also raised significant sums. Whatever the definition of 'large', and here I would take £6 million as a minimum, experience indicates that well planned and managed fundraising programmes will invariably raise more than appeals that tentatively seek funds out of desperation or speculation.

If there is a single fundamental ingredient to successful fundraising, it is to plan, review and plan again and thus to lay the most solid foundations possible. The following planning process will ensure that you are working towards a viable financial goal with appropriate resources in place:

- a comprehensive and compelling statement of needs
- adequate financial, administrative and organizational structures
- skilled and motivated staff
- an appropriate volunteer network
- a pool of relevant prospective donors
- a managerial structure to ensure that the plan can be implemented and progress monitored
- the total commitment and dynamic participation of the chief executive.

The campaign plan must focus upon identifying prospective donors, researching their interests, understanding their current and potential relationship with the institution and identifying their reasons for making donations. It is essential to understand what a potential donor would really like to achieve by making a charitable gift and to demonstrate how he or she can achieve this goal by supporting the institution.

The fundraising process

It is impossible to present the entire fundraising process in one chapter; nonetheless, some of the most important steps to be taken can be highlighted. The steps are described in a broadly sequential order but it is both necessary and desirable to revisit early assumptions and to develop and fine-tune them at each major step on the way. It is also important to bear in mind that, despite the emphasis on managing processes, a successful fundraising programme depends greatly on the ability to manage relationships and expectations, both within the institution and in the external world.

Where do I start?

There are three key stages within any fundraising initiative:

- planning and preparation
- active fundraising
- completion and stewardship.

All three stages must be carefully thought through at the outset; the policy and management decisions taken during the planning period will set the course of your fundraising programme. It is my belief that the most important element of the planning and preparation period is designing and implementing a feasibility study.

The feasibility study

A feasibility study will provide the first indication of whether your institution has the capability to raise 'large sums'. It will also suggest how much may be raised, whether the timing is right and how long it is likely to take. A comprehensive study will indicate appropriate leadership, suggest management and volunteer structures from both the internal and external communities, and provide an indication of how much the initial campaign cost and ongoing budget should be.

A focused and professionally managed feasibility study will form the heart of your campaign strategy and business plan. The process of conducting a feasibility study involves a number of interviews with, among others, those who may become donors. Questions will embrace the perception of the institution and whether financial support is likely to be given. In order to obtain full and frank views, it is preferable for the study to be conducted by an independent body.

Feasibility studies are not inexpensive, costing anywhere between £15,000 and £25,000, but this financial commitment is essential to future success. A higher education institution in the UK today cannot afford to miss the opportunity to boost income with charitable donations and must regard this initial outlay as a prerequisite for long-term rewards. The outcome of the study may also prevent expensive mistakes.

Commissioning a comprehensive feasibility study will establish the parameters for:

- identifying the needs of the institution and establishing priorities
- evaluating and establishing the financial context of the campaign
- assessing the availability of potential donors
- designing the fundraising strategy
- preparing the case for support
- establishing appropriate administrative, organizational and management structures.

Identification and prioritization of needs

Identifying the institution's needs and setting its priorities is a fundamental step in involving and obtaining the commitment of the university or college community. Inviting nominations from all departments for institution-wide as well as department-based projects will generate broad awareness, interest, enthusiasm and commitment to the campaign.

It is, however, important to employ transparent procedures for filtering and selecting priorities for campaign objectives. It is preferable to use known and respected consultative mechanisms to gather suggestions, and an ad hoc campaign planning board, comprising deans, student representatives and other interested parties, to make the final recommendations on funding priorities.

A portfolio containing a balance of general objectives such as 'scholarships', 'academic posts' or 'library resources' as well as department-specific objectives will be more attractive to potential donors than a portfolio that is either very narrowly focused or one that is too broad and does not identify priorities. A balance of 'general' and 'focused' objectives will also continue to engage the interest and support of those academics whose specific causes did not become part of the campaign portfolio.

Once the fundraising portfolio has been agreed, an internal campaign management committee should be appointed to:

- monitor progress
- agree the disbursement of funds
- take responsibility for adding or deleting projects from the portfolio
- authorize any shift in policy or strategy.

This group will not only protect the campaign staff from being overwhelmed by funding requests from departments but will also ensure that any additional fundraising objectives continue to support the institution's core development plan. It is essential that the chief executive officer is a member of this management group, in order to demonstrate his or her commitment to the campaign in the eyes of the institution as a whole as well as the external community.

Evaluating and establishing the financial context for the campaign

There are certain important financial factors to be taken into consideration in addition to the obvious questions, 'how much can I raise?' and 'what will it cost?' In broad terms, these are:

- the financial parameters of the campaign
- the management and disbursement of campaign income

- the general economic climate in the areas from which you aspire to raise funds.

Can I raise as much as I need?

There is often a discrepancy between the total costs of the objectives to be funded and the amount the feasibility study suggests could be raised. The results of the feasibility study will indicate whether you have been too ambitious or whether there is potential for even larger financial targets.

It is important to bear in mind that the size of the fundraising target itself can influence the amount raised; evidence suggests that a higher target stretches donors to make larger gifts than they would towards a lower one. Tax incentives for donors around the world should be explored and relevant information provided to potential donors.

Initially, the feasibility study should take into account the actual sum needed. This figure should be carefully crafted by ensuring that all overheads and on-costs have been taken into consideration. It is also important to determine whether the full cost of the project must be raised, where any balance of funds will be found, when the money is needed and whether phased contributions can be accepted. In addition, the potential effect on your public relations as well as the financial consequences of failing to meet any publicized campaign targets should be clearly understood by all concerned.

Responsibility for the management and disbursement of funds should also be clearly defined. It is also advisable for campaign accounting conventions and procedures to be agreed between development and finance personnel at the beginning of a campaign.

Assessing the availability of potential donors

Testing the water

Typically, the consultant conducting the feasibility study will construct a notional 'gift table' suggesting the number of gifts of various sizes needed to achieve the financial objective. This table will be based on the consultant's experience of the pattern of gifts made to comparable causes by categories of donors similar to those who might support your cause (see Table 11.1).

Once established, the gift table will be tested against the interest expressed or commitments given by those interviewed during the

Table 11.1   Notional gift table for a £6 million target

	Size of gift needed (gross value) £	Number of gifts needed	Number of prospects needed (4:1)	Total £	Cumulative total £
Leadership gifts	750,000	1	4	750,000	750,000
	500,000	2	8	1,000,000	1,750,000
	250,000	3	12	750,000	2,500,000
Major gifts	100,000	5	20	500,000	3,000,000
	50,000	5	20	250,000	3,250,000
	25,000	10	40	250,000	3,500,000
Special gifts	10,000	50	200	500,000	4,000,000
	5,000	100	400	500,000	4,500,000
	1,000	200	800	200,000	4,700,000
General gifts	up to 1,000	at least 1,300	5,200	1,300,000	6,000,000

feasibility study and against the perceived giving-capability of potential donors on your database. Once tested and refined, the gift table will provide an invaluable tool with which to evaluate progress throughout the campaign.

A word of warning. It is essential to have a large enough number of potential donors to call upon. Received wisdom indicates that three-quarters of 'asks' will fail. To succeed, you will need a large pool of potential donors with both affinity and affection for the institution and the financial capability of making the gifts required.

Who are my potential donors and where will I find them

The four main categories of potential major donors are typically:

- individuals
- companies
- charitable trusts and foundations
- other organizations such as professional associations.

Once the notional gift table has been constructed it is time to review the categories of potential donors more closely and to begin to put names into each category. The higher the goal, the greater the number of potential donors of large gifts that must be identified.

The construction of a database of 'relevant' prospective donors is a top priority. Relevance is important. There are many lists of individuals, companies and trusts available, with rankings according to perceived wealth or generosity. It is important to establish criteria for adding such information to your database. Relevant criteria would include:

- any existing relationship with the institution, e.g. as a former student, supplier, research contractor, recruiter of students, membership of the governing body, current student, parent or member of staff
- business interests in the region
- business or personal interests in the cause requiring funding
- a history of supporting similar causes
- a 'friend of the institution' in a position of influence over potential donors

A review and analysis of alumni records may identify potential major donors or potential emissaries (intermediaries) to potential donors. Conducting a biographical survey of alumni to capture employment and income data as well as information about current interests and links to the institution is worthwhile preparation for a campaign. This is one of the reasons why the fundraisers and alumni relations staff should share a common database and understand the importance of working closely together towards the achievement of the campaign goal.

I have thousands of names on my database – where do I start?

It is easy to be overwhelmed by the volume of data. It is important to divide the database into manageable subdivisions by sorting and coding donors according to notional wealth bands and arranging them further into groups according to 'warmth' factors, suggesting the propensity to give (see Table 11.2).

These subdivisions will help prioritize approaches to potential donors when the fundraising begins. This analysis will help to assess the number of prospective donors (prospects) available to make a gift at each level.

If you assume that, broadly speaking, four prospective donors will be needed for each gift required, it is easy to assess whether your database provides a sound enough foundation upon which to build your campaign, and how much 'cultivation' is needed to move

Table 11.2 Database subdivisions

Potential to give/net worth/ disposable income	Warmth towards cause/institution	Propensity to give	Suggested priority
High (income/giving bands 3–6)	High	A	1
High (income/giving bands 3–6)	Low	B	2
Low (income/giving bands 1–2)	High	C	3
Low (income/giving bands 1–2)	Low	D	4

prospective donors from 'cool' to 'warm'. The data will establish which particular fundraising strategy is needed and what level of resource is required.

The fundraising strategy

Successful fundraising depends upon careful planning and the strategic use of information and resources. There are many systems for establishing, guiding and monitoring the fundraising process, one of which focuses on seven I's, namely:

- Identifying the potential donors
- Informing them about the institution and its needs
- Involving them in the life or work of the institution
- Inspiring them to:
- Invest
- Inducting donors to an appropriate 'hall of fame'
- Iterating the process so that the donor continues to be involved and informed.

A pause is typically taken between each stage to evaluate what has been learned up to that point and to review the next step in the light of any new information received.

There should be a written, personalized, plan for the cultivation, solicitation and stewardship of each potential donor. The higher the gift sought, the more 'customized' the plan must be. In most instances, personal interaction is the most effective method of fundraising, with face-to-face meetings taking precedence over a telephone call.

Raising large gifts usually requires a longer-term strategy and a greater amount of personal interaction to set the stage for this level of giving. Depending on the warmth factor and size of gift sought, a major gift could take a number of years to come to fruition. Medium-sized gifts typically arise from two or three regular meetings with prospective donors to assess and discuss his or her inclination and motivation to give.

A particularly effective short-term strategy for contacting the generality of alumni is a telephone campaign. Gifts will normally be much smaller than those solicited face-to-face. The telephone call is, however, a successful medium for both establishing personal contact and generating a large number of gifts within a few months.

As a rule of thumb, a major gift officer can typically manage a portfolio of between 150 and 200 prospects. The number of major gifts needed and the number of potential major donors on a database will indicate the optimum number of major gift officers needed to achieve the campaign goal.

The role of volunteers

A successful fundraising strategy is one that involves volunteers. These are usually people who are:

- aware of the needs of the institution
- personally committed to its success
- prepared to make an early leadership gift
- willing to persuade others to do likewise.

Volunteers can unlock major gifts that staff cannot. They also influence major donors as well as lend considerable credibility to a campaign. To be most effective, volunteers must work strategically alongside paid personnel. They must be made aware that their commitment of both time and money is valued and that their advice is given due consideration.

It is important that volunteer boards have a clear remit and it should be explicitly stated at the outset whether or not they have executive as well as advisory responsibilities.

Establishing appropriate administrative and organizational structures

A successful fundraising programme requires organizational and management structures that can develop and deliver policy and strategy, and achieve goals on time and within budget.

The development office

It is advisable to establish a 'nuclear' development office at the earliest opportunity, for example when the decision to commission a feasibility study has been taken. There will be a need for staff to coordinate the provision of information for the study and to liaise with those conducting it.

Staff responsibilities will embrace:
• managing the planning and preparation activities
• developing and implementing fundraising policy and strategy
• servicing project committees
• researching prospective donors
• constructing budgets for ongoing future fundraising activities
• evaluating, purchasing and setting up specialist 'fundraising' databases
• acquiring appropriate IT equipment.

A core development office should comprise:
• a senior manager with knowledge and experience of fundraising, responsible for construction and implementation of strategy and major gifts
• a development services manager to set the administrative processes in place
• an alumni relations officer.
• prospect research staff
• data input staff
• clerical/secretarial support
• a gift officer

Fundraising staff should be recruited as soon as it is apparent that the institution will embark upon a fundraising initiative. It is preferable for fundraisers to be recruited early in the planning period so that they will be involved in the preparation of the case statement and become acquainted with the structures, ethos, history and leading personalities of the institution as well as with prospective and current donors.

The institution should plan for the phased expansion of the development office. The deployment of staff will alter throughout the life of the campaign to reflect adjustments to fundraising priorities and to concentrate upon the more productive sources of gifts.

As the fundraising programme achieves success, academic units will wish to participate more intensely. There are two ways of addressing this situation. One is to allocate responsibility for all funding objectives for one or more academic units to specific fundraisers within the development office. The second is for each academic unit to have its own fundraising staff. Whichever model is employed, it is of critical importance that there is central coordination of approaches to prospective donors and a central overview of institution-wide funding objectives.

Large gifts can be realized if fundraising staff are experienced in cultivating donors and soliciting major gifts, and are self-motivated and proactive in initiating contact with donors. In the UK, there is a growing body of experienced and skilled fundraising personnel. There are, however, still too few to meet the demands of a growing market. Many recruits will, therefore, need to receive basic training 'on the job' and through professional organizations such as the Council for the Advancement and Support of Education (CASE), and the Institute of Charity Fundraising Managers (ICFM). There is also an increasing number of consultants offering training.

Budget

Large sums will be raised if the institution is willing to invest in an appropriate number of qualified staff, to fund a comprehensive and ambitious fundraising programme and to provide the appropriate administrative infrastructure. Data from the United States indicate that a campaign may cost between 15 and 20 per cent of the target. When setting the budget, it is worth remembering that those capable of making donations of millions of pounds respect and expect professionalism and quality.

Accountability

There is a growing demand for accountability in all areas of the institution's activities. The fundraising process is a high investment and there should, therefore, be a clear control and review process attached to the expenditure of the operating budget, and to the recording and distribution of gift income, to satisfy both internal and external audit requirements.

Fundraising staff should also be held accountable for their activities. The establishment and agreement of individual as well as team goals, and the confirmation of performance indicators will become as commonplace in the UK as they are in the United States. Core measurement criteria will include:

- the estimated number of gifts needed to achieve the overall target
- the number of visits/contacts needed to generate a gift
- the number of visits a fundraiser is expected to make each month or each year
- the number and average size of gifts to be generated in any given period.

Inter-related strategies

The fundraising strategy resides at the heart of any development campaign. It should, however, be supported by the administrative procedures referred to above and complemented by an alumni relations programme and a marketing plan. This plan ensures that there are formal and informal communications networks in place between the potential donors and the institution, and also between relevant departments. The marketing plan will support the development of:

- a strong case statement – the detailed rationale for the fundraising initiatives
- compelling campaign publications
- complementary alumni publications and events
- a policy to ensure that the institution acknowledges and publicizes gifts
- a donor relations policy that will include a programme of events and visits for individual potential donors as well as for large and small groups, both on and off campus. Each event must be designed to move a prospective donor, or group of donors, along the campaign path.

The fundraising phase of the campaign

This phase will be divided into two parts. The first will be a private phase during which initial gifts are sought. It is usual to raise 25–33 per cent of the financial target in a private phase of the campaign in order to test the target and to send the message that the campaign is on track to succeed. When this is achieved, the campaign should be launched with as much publicity as possible.

It is during the fundraising phase that the sources of income will be closely monitored to ensure that fundraising staff are being deployed most effectively.

At the end of the road

The final phase of any fundraising campaign should be concerned with:

- thanking donors, volunteers and staff
- celebrating successes
- raising gifts that were initiated but not realized during the campaign period
- continuing to inform donors and prospective donors about the institution
- planning and managing the transition period from the end of one campaign period to the start of another
- maintaining motivation and momentum within all fundraising, alumni relations, public relations and marketing functions
- evaluating processes, structures, personnel and sources of income thereby laying the ground for raising even larger sums next time.

In conclusion

By this stage you will have formed a view on whether your institution might be able to raise large gifts and have a better idea of how to conduct the process. As emphasized, the most beneficial investment of time is at an early stage: in the planning and preparation period during which a feasibility study should be commissioned and evaluated. Each university has the potential to raise large gifts, provided that there is an appropriate commitment of both time and financial resources.

12

WELL CONNECTED
Organizational structure

**Frank Albrighton and
Julia Thomas**

The University of California at Davis has one hundred professional staff engaged in external relations. This is according to the directory of the Council for Advancement and Support of Education (CASE) which has a membership of many thousands of what are known as 'advancement professionals' in North America.[1] The complement at California is large, but it is not extraordinary.

The Californian team includes 22 members of staff who have the title 'director'. There is a director of development, a director of the news service, a director of advancement services and a director of government and community relations. There is also a director of donor assets planning, a director of chapter development and (chillingly, when you remember what it means) a director of planned giving.

In 1998 the author Hunter Davies wrote an article called 'Born 1900' in 'The Birmingham Magazine', which is the alumni magazine of the University of Birmingham.[2] The article was based on research Davies had conducted for a book of the same name that celebrated people born and institutions established in 1900, including the university.

In the Birmingham article he talked about visiting the university to find out about the modern campus. In paying tribute to the help he had received he said:

> The University's Director of Communications was also jolly help-
> ful. Did you know she existed? Not to mention the Depart-
> ment of External Relations and Development...
> When I was a student there were no such PR animals. Now
> every university has them or similar.

It is interesting that even now an observer in the UK should find it
worthwhile to comment on the existence of PR animals in a university. He is right, of course, that all universities have them. The UK
equivalent of the CASE directory is the HEERA (Higher Education
External Relations Association) *List of Members*.[3] Not surprisingly,
this is a much slimmer volume than its American counterpart. A
glance through this publication reveals that the high scores come
from places like the University of Westminster which lists 18 staff,
and King's College, London, which has 15. These are large offices by
UK standards, even allowing for the vagaries of the way people
submit entries to such publications. At the other end of scale, UMIST
in Manchester, which is a prestigious university, lists only two external relations professionals. So Hunter Davies is right: there are PR
animals prowling all over the higher education jungle. Sometimes
they hunt – or defend themselves – in a pack; sometimes they are
solitary raiders.

Interestingly, although UMIST boasts only a small PR department
it was one of the first higher education institutions in the UK to
have a full-time professional information officer. The origin of the
activity in the UK can be traced back to the troubled times of the
late 1960s when students were engaged in protest across the world.
The events of Paris in May 1968 had their rather more muted counterparts in the UK. There was never any likelihood of governments
being toppled or workers striking in support of students, but some
university senates became very agitated and a few people thought
that student power was the end of civilization as we knew it. The
sit-ins, protests, marches, and all the rest had a immediate effect on
the external relations business. Barricaded buildings and waving
anarchist flags very quickly caught the attention of the media. For
the first time, universities found that their actions were splashed across
the popular press in a way to which they were totally unaccustomed.
Until then, 'University News' was a listing of appointments and other
routine information in the *Times*. The *Times Higher Education Supplement* had not even been launched.

University campuses found themselves visited by journalists who
wanted a good story, reporters who would talk to articulate and media-
friendly students, and photographers who recorded the drama of
hundreds of students chanting, marching and besieging administrative

headquarters. In most universities until then, the job of dealing with the media – little more than issuing good news press releases – had fallen to one of the members of the central administration as part of a range of general duties, not as a specialism.

There is an apocryphal story of one registrar who surveyed the baying pack of media waiting to hear his explanation of the university's latest capitulation to student demands. He commented *sotto voce* to a colleague, 'This is no job for a gentleman. We need an information officer'.

And so the noble profession of external relations in British universities was born. The initial impetus was to find people who could cope with, if not, in those early days, manipulate the media. That suggested that people with a journalistic background or at least with good journalistic skills would be required. Once those skills made themselves felt in the universities it was short step to apply them to other areas of work, especially publications. Quite quickly the typical information office was responsible for media relations, publications like prospectuses and for general public relations advice to institutions that had not before felt the need. That is not quite the whole story, because vice-chancellors have always performed a representative role and have been acutely aware of the effect of public opinion on the welfare of their institutions. For the first time, though, the glare of publicity and demands of public accountability were felt across the whole institution.

Over the ensuing thirty years, information officers and their successors never lost that key role of dealing with the media. It is still seen as no job for a gentleman and it is probably the one area of external relations work, especially in times of crisis, where colleagues do not feel that they could do the job just as well, and probably better, themselves, if only they had time. As the job has grown and changed, former journalists are now in the minority. Communication skills are still crucial, but even more so is the ability to operate successfully in complex organizations, relating to a wide range of constituencies, both internal and external, using the whole range of communications techniques of which media relations is just one.

Other than in media relations, the roles and priorities of information officers have changed a good deal. In different institutions at different times there have been changes of preoccupations so that at one time media relations is the most important work and at another it is student recruitment. More recently, fundraising has become in many places the most important part of external relations work and the most generously resourced. When, in the 1980s, the Conservative government told the universities that it was time 'to get out the begging bowl' it was received with horror by the external relations professionals at the time. This was not what external relations was about, it was not how universities ought to be funded and, in any case, although it might be appropriate for the United States, it would not work here.

Now development is an important part of the external relations work of the majority of higher education institutions. In one way or another it is linked closely to all external relations activities, and the culture of helping income generation in the broadest sense pervades all the external relations work of a modern office. This is reflected in the titles and descriptions used in the various offices listed in the HEERA directory. No one is called an information officer now, but we see words like marketing, corporate affairs, communications, development and external relations used in many different combinations, reflecting the organization and the culture of the individual institutions.

Thinking of the issues that face higher education institutions in the twenty-first century, many of them closely linked to their relations with external organizations and individuals, is there an ideal organizational structure for external relations? Probably not. But there are some important principles that ought to be applied, whatever detailed structure a particular institution chooses to adopt.

Writing as long ago as 1987, Clive Keen and John Greenall said:

There are a number of ways of structuring the PR operations of a college, and because of the different circumstances of each college, the desirable approach is to create a structure which groups together as many as possible of the cognate fields, e.g.: advertising, alumni affairs, ceremonials, fund-raising, graphics, industrial liaison, internal communications, marketing, media liaison, parliamentary liaison, publications, reprographics, schools liaison, visits.

A unit comprising all, or most, of these functions could be brought together by a single individual with responsibility for the broad area, though various line managers might remain responsible for the day-to-day tasks. A number of colleges have made a step in this direction by appointing a 'head of external relations' at a senior level to oversee the broad area, and it is encouraging that a few colleges have recently adopted the most appropriate system of all, which is to appoint to the directorate a specialist in public relations, corporate affairs and marketing. Such a move is analogous to the increasing trend in British industry and commerce to appoint a director of public relations at boardroom level.[4]

Although this does now have a slightly old-fashioned ring to it, the principles are remarkably similar to those advocated nowadays by, for example, Larry Lauer writing on integrated marketing strategy elsewhere in this book. The key principle of the organization is that it must facilitate the consistent presentation of a series of clear institutional messages to all the institution's audiences. Because, as we have hinted earlier, external relations is prey to the intervention and prejudices of a wide number of people, it is essential that the activity has support and policy direction from the highest possible level in the institution. This means that external relations policies must have the personal commitment, if not the day-to-day involvement, of the head of the institution. In some places this will be delegated to a deputy or the head of the administration, but they too must be sure that they are operating with clear and unswerving institutional support. This is because external relations policies must be dedicated to supporting the interest of the institution itself. They must be above all sectional interests. Obviously, promotional work and other activities find expression through the achievements and activities of academic and administrative departments, but the external relations policies and practices must derive from the overarching policies of the institution. This matters if you are to get the big picture right and sharply in focus. But it will also matter when there are niggling but important disputes about the manifestations and implementation of those policies. These could be to do with policing of visual identity, managing negative press publicity or making sure that visitors are properly and courteously received.

At the level below this stratospheric endorsement there are many ways of getting your act together. The marketing taskforce, bringing together disparate groups across the institution, is one way of doing it. Keen and Greenall talked about a single officer having responsibility across a wide range of duties and this has indeed been the case in a number of institutions, especially the so-called post-1992 universities. As in any other area of management, personalities, personal attitudes and preferences will also play a part. But however you set it up, wherever you draw the dividing lines between the different activities, you must ensure that there is effective integration and a common sense of purpose. The more dividing lines you have, the less likely you are to achieve this as office politics and turf wars get in the way.

There are some places where you really should not make a separation. One of these is between development and alumni. There are a thousand good reasons why an institution should cultivate a good relationship with its alumni, and most of them have nothing to do with fundraising. They include assistance with student recruitment, with links with industry, with career mentoring, with the media, with politics, and many others. But the political reality is that sooner or later an institution will need to justify its investment in its alumni relations work by undertaking fundraising. When that happens the close relationship between the fundraisers and the alumni relations staff is paramount. They above all must share a common strategy and organizational role or the fundraising will be hampered and relationships with alumni will be damaged.

You should have very good reasons to separate the media and public relations work from the production of the principal publications. Advertising and public relations are effective through repetition, simplicity and consistency. You need the same ideas, even the same phrases and the same images, to be appearing in the media and your main publications. Publications nowadays include those on the web and the demarcation between print and electronic is daily becoming more and more blurred. If you have an internal graphic design service then that should be locked into both of these to ensure visual consistency and high quality design. If those who produce publications, printed and electronic, are not subjected to the discipline and quality standards of professional graphic designers, then quality and effectiveness will diminish.

The term 'marketing' is used increasingly, not always with a full awareness of what it means, and so we have marketing departments who in industrial parlance are really sales departments since they have no influence on the products that they are offering to customers. There are signs that this is changing, however, and true marketing is beginning to find its place in higher education. As this happens and there is an increasing emphasis on market research, it argues again for close integration. The market research that tells you whether a particular academic programme would be attractive will also tell you what points to emphasize to potential students and how to present them. This suggests that marketing, usually with an emphasis on student recruitment, should work closely with publications.

It is easily possible to continue this line of argument and arrive back at the Keen and Greenall solution whereby everything is under one roof. Realism and pragmatism suggest that in most cases this will not be achievable and may indeed be inappropriate. But the principal of integration and coordination is essential.

One area of the organization is a bit special and this again concerns media relations. It may be that the head of external relations is also the principal press officer, or that may be a duty delegated to others. There are some special requirements for anyone who has the job of speaking to the press on the institution's behalf, especially but not exclusively in times of crisis. First of all you need to decide who has the authority to give that type of institutional comment. Reactions to events will be sought virtually every day and it is important that there is absolute clarity about which members of the institution may speak on its behalf. Clearly, the chief executive has that authority and he or she is likely to delegate it to deputies and to the head of the administration. Beyond that, there should one or two members of the external relations staff whose names are known to the media as people having authority to give on-the-record press statements and interviews. This, incidentally, will inevitably subject them to constant out-of-hours telephone calls. It is a matter for consideration whether this should be formalized into some kind of rota system.

There is another important requirement for an effective press liaison activity. The press officer must be given access to all the information possible. He or she should attend the meetings of governing bodies and other key committees. It is no substitute to be briefed by someone who was present at the meeting. A good reporter will have a lot of information about controversial events and the press officer must be briefed just as well. It can be disastrous if the press officer is briefed by a senior member of the institution on what they would like to appear in the newspaper. The story must be shared with the press officer, warts and all. It is then a matter for discussion and judgement to decide how this story is presented to the media.

In some institutions, especially other parts of the public sector, there are strict controls which prohibit virtually any member of staff, other than the press officer, from speaking to the media. Many universities, however, are happy for individual members of the academic staff to speak to the media in their area of expertise. They may encourage this by publishing lists of experts who are available to give comment on topical events. The view is taken that in speaking on an academic matter the reputation at stake is not so much that of the institution but of the individual academic. In that sense it is no different from publishing a paper or a book, although the consequences can be more rapid and publicly spectacular.

This leads to the question of control of who says what. The University of Birmingham has dealt with this by producing a code of practice on publications and communications (see Appendix) that is binding on all members of staff. The origin of this was that a few years ago there was a high profile court case where a member of university staff was charged and eventually sentenced for offences concerning pornographic material and the internet. Not surprisingly, this troubled the university and it was decided that, with the advent of the unprecedented world wide communications power of the internet, there had to be some explicit regulation within the university of what could be done and by whom. The culture of the Internet, in its early years in particular, was one of completely free expression, unfettered, unhindered and uncensored. The code of practice was devised to make, first of all, a distinction between academic publishing – where individual members of staff are accountable to their peers for their own reputations – and any publications, printed or electronic, that either are or could be perceived as carrying the authority of the university as an institution. The code allocates different levels of editorial control, ranging from publications where control is total, as in the case of recruitment prospectuses, to other publications where the attitude of the university will be more relaxed. The Birmingham code is now in need of some revision as legislation concerning freedom of information, data protection and human rights impinges upon it, but the principle of demonstrating clearly to staff what are their responsibilities to the institution and how they will be held accountable is still an important one.

Once you have established your external relations team and their relationships to each other you must think about their relationship to the rest of the university. These days you could not possibly say otherwise than that they must be customer-led. But who is the customer? Is it the public? Is it the media? Is it the external constituencies? Or is it the vice-chancellor or the departments that come along and want various services? Is the external relations department there to provide a service or to influence policy? These are not issues for which there is a simple prescription because once again they will be influenced by the culture and conditions of the individual institution, but they are points that the higher management and the leadership of the external relations function itself should consider as they decide how to create an effective organization.

Notes

1 Council for Advancement and Support of Education (2000) *Membership Directory*. Washington, DC: CASE.
2 University of Birmingham (1998) *The Birmingham Magazine*.
3 Higher Education External Relations Association (1999) *List of Members*. London: HEERA.
4 C. Keen and J. Greenhall (1987) *Public Relations Management in Colleges, Polytechnics and Universities*. Bradford: HEIST, p.94.

13

ALL TOGETHER NOW
A strategic institutional approach to integrated marketing

Larry D. Lauer

Integrated marketing is a strategic approach to advancing colleges and universities that ultimately seeks to involve everyone in the institution in attracting good students, raising money and enhancing visibility. It leads to more focused institutional goals and to getting everyone 'on the same page' with respect to the institution's competitive advantage and unique strengths.

Why now?

Recent experience suggests that there are four immediate reasons to implement integrated marketing which are shared by colleges and universities around the world. These are:

- an intense increase in the competition for students
- more sophisticated consumers asking more questions and demanding more 'quality'
- more fundraising campaigns competing for donor loyalty
- a demand by institutional stakeholders for more public visibility.

These are pretty much the same factors around the world, even though the social, cultural and institutional dynamics surrounding them are often different.

How does integrated marketing relate to higher education?

In higher education it is of paramount importance that everyone should understand that integrated marketing is *a way of thinking*, not a way of commercializing. It is a way of understanding the needs of students and making certain that programmes and services meet those needs. It is a way of thinking about all aspects of the enterprise at the same time: consumer or student needs, the programmes and services which meet those needs, the way communication takes place, the way the services are delivered, and the price that is charged. Commercializing comes only in the way these things are carried out, and it is not necessary to commercialize to advance most institutions of higher education.

First, integrated marketing is a way of bringing decentralized departments together in order to maximize impact. It either sets up a team of people across organizational boundaries or it suggests organizational alternatives in order to achieve marketing coordination.

Next, integrated marketing seeks to mobilize talent, resources and leadership in order to maximize impact. It seeks out people with marketing interests and skills no matter where they are in the organization and brings them together to make the most of available financial and other resources. This means that integrated marketing focuses on organizational goals. It avoids planning around the political interests and benefits of departmental units and sets up a process whereby the priorities of the organization drive the priorities of marketing and communications.

Integrated marketing, therefore, insists that public relations, advertising and other marketing initiatives be planned together as one coordinated campaign. This eliminates discussions about which of these is more effective; it also eliminates media placement decisions which are driven more by the 'pitches' of media salespeople than by the institution's strategic plan. Integrated marketing definitely asserts that all communications tools are effective and that the best one for each situation should be used.

Further, integrated marketing asserts that an institution's loyal relationships are its best competitive advantage. Therefore it seeks to use a variety of interactive communications tactics to build those relationships and prefers them to traditional mass communications tactics.

Overall, the objective of integrated marketing is to get everyone in the institution 'on the same page'. Everyone should understand the institution's mission, vision and values. Everyone should be able to explain its market niche and its competitive advantages. And everyone should understand their responsibility to help tell the story – and to find students, raise money and lift visibility.

Developing a model at Texas Christian University ▮

In my own institution, Texas Christian University, we are developing a task force-based model for integrated marketing. It is founded on the realization that changing the structure of the institution to establish a marketing division was not feasible as it could not include in it every department that should be included. And so we created a marketing advisory board to bring into conversation with us about goals everyone who had a stake in marketing inside the institution as well as a few from outside. Members ranged from the admissions dean to the bookstore manager to the assistant vice-chancellor for student affairs. The outside members included an alumnus who owns an advertising agency and the president of the chamber of commerce. From this group a smaller management committee of nine members was established to commission research and make final action decisions, and four even smaller action groups to carry out specific initiatives in student recruiting, institutional visibility, internal communications, athletics marketing and advancement participation. The lessons learned from integrated marketing in this manner and from travels to other campuses are reflected in what follows.

Transforming institutions ▮

The most important lesson is that transforming an institution is a much more comprehensive job than designing a major public relations or communications campaign. And a transforming mindset is critical to launching a new marketing initiative. All of the communications materials in the world will only produce a temporary public notice of an institution. A true transformation requires that an institution's major constituencies perceive a fundamental movement forward, and that the forward movement is seen in the behaviours of its central leadership.

Transforming institutions, therefore, requires not only an integrated approach to marketing, but also a dynamic strategic plan that clarifies mission, vision and values, and a leadership group which is out front, visible and inspirational. And these leaders must establish a team-building, process-oriented management style in the total organization.

Team-building requires getting people out of their boxes so they can think more freely. Creativity and innovation are critical factors.

The bottom line is that institutions that attract positive public attention today must be seen to have bold ideas. An effective marketing programme must therefore be a part of an overall institutional transformation initiative.

Marketing higher education as a way of thinking ▮

The task of integrated marketing professionals is to translate the latest thinking in the dynamic field of marketing to the setting of higher education. Traditionally, the field of marketing has been characterized by what is referred to as the 4 Ps – product, price, place and promotion – plus several other concepts which include segmentation and positioning.

Product

In higher education the concept of product should be viewed on two levels. First, to what degree is the experience of the institution itself the product the consumer buys? The answer to this question varies from institution to institution. In most cases, identifying and clarifying an institution's products involves seeing both the overall educational experience as one level of product and the various degree programmes as another. Both levels should be clarified and then understood by everyone in the institution. And then the various degree programmes must be analysed with respect to which ones define the institution.

In general, in smaller institutions it is more likely that overall image and curricular experience will be the primary perceived product. In the case of larger institutions, it is more likely that specific programmes combined with perceptions of brand significance will shape what the consumer thinks he or she is buying. Bringing the entire institution to a clear understanding of these distinctions is the challenge of the product analysis part of integrated marketing. The key is *positioning* the institution so that it and its products are differentiated from the competition.

The issue of *quality* is also an important part of product understanding. In higher education, as in many other industries, the perception of quality is the only one that will sell. But what determines the perception of quality? In many cases an institution is seen as having quality merely because it is difficult to gain admittance to it, and so selectivity based on intelligence has been seen as the most important quality indicator. But today's more sophisticated consumer is asking 'quality' questions about faculty credentials, teaching quality, personal attention, job placement and personal amenities, and so answering quality-related questions is becoming more complicated for those in higher education leadership roles.

Price

Price is possibly the most complicated part of the marketing equation, particularly in higher education. In some countries, especially the United States, there is a growing sense that the general public feels that higher education institutions have 'outpriced' themselves, while some clearly still feel that if the price is not high the product cannot be good. In addition, the general practice of using financial aid and scholarships as discounting tools has increased public confusion.

In pricing, there must be a balance between the cost to the consumer and the perceived value of the product or service received in exchange. Each industry seems to have its own set of factors that influence and shape that perceived balance. In higher education, consumer perceptions vary, from the belief that an education should be virtually free to the feeling that the price should always be high but that no one should actually pay it. In the final analysis, the higher education market all over the world seems to have consumers with varying perceptions about what the price ought to be. Consequently, selecting a price and 'discounting' philosophy becomes one area of important competitive differentiation.

The shape of this pricing issue is also different from country to country. In the UK, for example, where higher education has been virtually free of charge in the past, the recent addition of a uniform tuition payment and the anticipation of eventual pricing differentiation adds an important marketing factor for each institution to analyse.

Place

The word 'place' in marketing refers to methods of product distribution. In higher education, clarifying the concept of distribution requires analysing the campus life experience, how education is delivered in the classroom, the relationship of satellite campuses to the main campus, and the use of technology.

There are three key concerns. First, to what extent do campus experiences and services affect consumer choice? Each student tends to think that each institution he or she considers has a high academic reputation and so the final choice is often based on other factors, such as location, convenience, housing quality, recreational opportunities and sports facilities. This realization can change dramatically how an institution is communicated.

Second, does the difference between the physical place and the experienced place affect college choice? There is often a big difference between what the campus actually looks like and how an individual experiences it. The 'experienced place' is shaped by all those relationships that are formed during the communication process and campus visits. Shaping the experienced place therefore becomes an important marketing goal.

Third, to what extent will the electronic revolution change how education is delivered? In other words, to what extent will residential-based education survive the Internet? Most believe that there will always be a market for residential campuses but that the Internet will change the size of that market and it will also change how education is delivered on those campuses. Being knowledgeable about and utilizing technology will be a critical component in developing competitive advantage and understanding the role of 'place' in marketing higher education.

Promotion

Promotion has traditionally referred to the role of communication in the marketing process, and new technologies and tactics are transforming how we think about communication today. The word 'promotion' no longer comes close to being adequate. In fact, most marketers today talk about promotion as really being 'integrated marketing communication', which requires segmenting the audience into groups which can be communicated with more precisely and directly.

Integrated marketing communications

New thinking about how communication works in marketing has revolutionized how many organizations' communications departments function. Today, 'the talk' is about the death of mass communications and the appearance of one-to-one relationship-building and communicating directly with market segments. Internet and digital technology is what is making that kind of thinking possible.

The concept is that when an organization achieves competitive advantage by introducing a new product, a compelling price or a new distribution convenience the competition will soon meet it and the competitive advantage vanishes. But when an organization achieves a loyal customer the competitive advantage continues indefinitely because people feel secure in trusting relationships and would prefer to do business where they can assume they will have them. Consequently, the most effective marketing communication activities will focus on identifying high potential customers and communicating with them as directly and interactively as possible.

This understanding will change how professional communicators spend their time. Offices of communications in universities will move away from a primary focus on news media relations which aims to achieve mentions for the institution in the press. This practice in the past often resulted in either disappointing coverage or in coverage that the right people never noticed. The integrated marketer will rather spend time identifying potential customers, important institutional stakeholders and community opinion leaders, and communicate directly and interactively with them.

These offices therefore will seek to change how they are perceived inside the organization. They will organize along the lines of an internal agency that helps internal programmes and event organizers to develop and launch comprehensive strategic communication campaigns. The office and its practitioners will seek to be seen as the experts who can combine public relations, advertising and other marketing tactics to build relationships with those who control the health and future of the institution: prospective students, alumni, donors and community leaders. This change may well be the most significant and productive one for colleges and universities to result from an understanding of integrated marketing.

Branding ■

The concept of branding refers to the power of name identity in the marketing of institutions. Recent experience indicates that the power of brand names to influence consumer behaviour is enormous. Indeed, some feel that consumers equate recognizability of brand name with quality of product, so that the better that an institution's name is known, the better its product is believed to be.

The implications of this are enormous for higher education communicators. But, how can institutions afford to become a household name? Indeed, it is likely that most colleges and universities will not be able to achieve this. Here again the concept of segmentation is critical. Maybe an institution cannot have its name on the tip of everyone's tongue, but it can become a brand of choice within targeted segments of the population. Thus, branding strategies are becoming a part of what integrated marketing is bringing to higher education.

Logos and design, the use of colours and sounds, all are becoming an important part of establishing higher education identity and visibility. Schools and colleges within universities can be viewed as sub-brands, and programmes as brand extensions – all concepts which help administrators to see how to coordinate the look and positioning of academic structures which require their own identity and yet need to be seen as a unified part of the whole.

New focus on research

It is embarrassing to think that most academic institutions which consider themselves to be teaching and research organizations do little research about their own marketplace. And when such research has been done in the past, it has taken the form of a comprehensive and expensive survey which ends up only confirming what the administration thought to be the case.

Market segmentation today, however, makes polling and focus group research more effective and affordable. Segmentation allows more precise questions to be asked of fewer people at less cost. Also, today's interactive communication technology allows feedback (or answers to research questions) to be built into the communication process itself. So, research is becoming more of a regular and ongoing part of the total marketing activity.

This segmented approach to research allows the testing of materials with specific groups, the development of effective positioning phrases, and an understanding of how institutional attitudes change and evolve over time with every important stakeholder group.

The experience of one old and established university in Canada provides a good example. This university set out to clarify its market identity largely in response to a local university's new president who was getting a lot of highly visible attention and money for an institution which had been largely invisible in the past. The older university has campuses in two cities, but this challenge for attention was centred in one of the cities only. This situation generated some segment-based identity research which revealed that, as the campus in the 'second city' gradually established its own identity, the identity for the overall institution became less clear, and as a result it was perceived as falling behind. This gave the new president of a rival institution the opportunity to gain the upper hand at least for the moment. Gradually what had been one university with two campuses had become two separate institutions over a period of years. It was clear to the researchers and consultants that competitive effectiveness could be regained for each one only if they separated.

Launching integrated marketing ∎

The objective of integrated marketing is to mobilize talent and re-sources, and this cannot be done without the up-front leadership of top administration. The first task is to get the president and cabinet on board, and this will require someone with experience and cred-ibility to meet them and answer their questions. This person may be inside the institution, but usually he or she is not. The usual approach is that a group inside the institution perceive the need and bring in someone from outside to meet with all the key players – the president, executives, deans, and other administrative staff and faculty, including the admissions staff, development staff, communications staff, alumni staff, and anyone else who will be affected by, or can contribute to, a marketing programme.

The basic question is: do you restructure the organization to bring all marketing-related functions into one division, or do you create an interdepartmental task force reporting to the president that accom-plishes the same result? Most institutions will choose the task force.

The task force will first need to find a 'champion' inside the organization to lead the charge and a consultant outside that can help solve problems. The champion needs to have a thorough under-standing of the marketing subject matter and have the respect of the faculty and administration. The consultant needs more than knowledge of marketing. He or she should have experience with solving the political and process problems of implementation inside a college or university.

Certain barriers will have to be overcome. First, the institution will have to come to see marketing as a way of thinking which not only does not cheapen the academy but actually raises some ser-ious quality-related questions to be addressed. Second, people in the institution will have to accept that this 'way of thinking' involves more than improving what is communicated: it also requires a ser-ious examination of products, pricing and distribution. Third, middle managers and administrators will have to give up turf battles so that inter-office teams can be formed and new initiatives launched. All of this will require top administrative leadership. And fourth, every-one in the institution will have to grant situational leadership to the 'champion', so that facilitation can work and concerns about political power can be put aside.

Integrated marketing and student recruiting ▮

The purpose of an integrated marketing task force is not to run the offices of admissions, public relations, fundraising, athletics, alumni offices, etc. on a daily basis, but rather to identify new initiatives, talent and resources which can bring better focus and intensity to the work of those offices. Therefore, integrated marketing people tend to concentrate on communication messages and materials audits, reviews of the total student prospect contact calendar, profiling current students, analysing current and potential market segments and focusing on the variables which most influence final choice.

The basic lessons learned are:

- it is easier and more cost effective to find more students like those you have than to open up whole new markets
- a complete analysis and fine-tuning of the communication process can bring very good results.

Lessons about visibility ▮

The central marketing question about an institution's visibility is: visibility with whom and at what cost? Colleges and universities cannot afford total visibility with everyone, so it is critical that those who control the health and future of the institution be identified. If these people can come to feel that the institution is well known, then for all practical purposes it really is. This is the 'strategic' solution to the visibility problem. Integrated marketing then brings new tactics to the table. First, the office of communications takes on educating faculty, staff and other stakeholders about the realities of the news business. They must come to understand that the business of news organizations is to advance their own goals and not yours. And so it is only when an institution's goals correspond with theirs that the institution will get satisfactory coverage of its positive stories. It is much more effective to send positive stories directly to those who need to see them.

Second, direct communication with stakeholders and opinion leaders will build bonded relationships with them, and this provides the best competitive advantage in student recruiting and fundraising. Students ultimately choose to attend the school they have developed the strongest relationship with during the recruiting process, and donors are more loyal to the campaigns of institutions they care the most about. A donor who loves a college or university, a symphony organization, a theatre, a museum, and an opera will become a more loyal donor to the organization that cultivates a bonded relationship.

Some universities are experimenting with special interest groups to broaden alumni participation and to establish more loyal relationships based on personal interests. The idea is that, using the Internet, the institution can facilitate the gathering of self-directed groups around any number of topics, no matter how small or how obscure. They can first chat on the Net and then arrange meetings and programmes on their own. The important ingredient is to encourage faculty and staff to join these groups so that alumni and donors experience these relationships and know that their institution made this personally satisfying enrichment possible.

Advertising is also usually seen differently when it is a part of an integrated marketing programme. Instead of putting advertisements in all of the usual places – education sections of newspapers or magazines allegedly read by young people – advertising is placed for one of two strategic purposes. First, advertising is placed for branding, or name recognition, in media that target specific audience segments. This kind of advertising focuses on name and image impact, not on detailed messages. Second, advertising is placed with a specific role to play within a larger strategic communication campaign. For example, during the time that prospective students are receiving direct mail about a college, the college may take an advertisement targeting the students' parents which addresses directly the parents' interests and concerns.

Texas Christian University (TCU) is experimenting with this kind of marketing-campaign-related advertising. Institutional messages have been placed in a high-circulation state-wide magazine which are designed to get opinion leaders (some of whom are likely to be parents of prospective students) to say: 'Wow, I didn't know TCU was doing that!' The advertising appears in this magazine at around the same time as direct mail is coming into the homes of prospective students and as student recruiters are visiting the high schools in the state.

Integrated marketing also uses the formation of partnerships as a way to address specific segments and bring instant recognition and visibility to a college or university. Partnerships work well in the areas of special events and programming. For example, an institution might sponsor a major art exhibit with an important museum and gain immediate visibility and stature. Or a social work degree programme might announce a major relationship with the largest human service agency in the area. Or a study abroad programme may forge a travel agreement with a major airline. All of these partnerships have the potential for both high visibility and reputation enhancement – if the partnering organization also has recognized prestige in the community or larger marketplace.

Lessons for alumni and development programmes

Most fundraising offices tend to organize donors according to donation levels and refer to them as members of related 'donor clubs'. This works pretty well for many institutions and has helped raise a lot of money, but it does not apply the full relationship-building potential of integrated marketing.

Integrated marketing suggests that stronger relationships can be developed through targeting alumni and donor interests – in business, art, music, and so on. Donors can be involved by being invited to give lectures, be a part of arts celebrations, attend lectures in their professional fields, and so forth. Most alumni associations target social interests pretty well through parties, receptions and athletic events, but here, too, other personal and professional interests are not capitalized upon. The integrated marketing programme sets out to bridge the gaps by involving the entire institution in building relationships with donors and alumni.

This kind of integrated approach also involves donors in the development of case statements for major fundraising campaigns before they are printed, thus achieving buy-in long before the campaign is announced. And integrated marketing tends to see the alumni relationship to the institution as a continuing life cycle, so that alumni children are communicated with from birth to college choice, and alumni themselves have a true life-long relationship, which includes access to the total resources and help of the institution. In this way, integrated marketing actually aims to make the institution as self-sustaining as possible, through a growing, loyal donor base and qualified alumni children choosing to continue the legacy.

Integrated marketing and strategic planning

Integrated marketing must be a part of the total planning of the institution because it is based on the premise that product, price, place and promotion must all be coordinated in order to make the institution viable in the marketplace. It is also based on the premise that decentralized departments must be coordinated and messages must be fine-tuned in order to maximize the effectiveness of the institution in the marketplace. To that end, a participatory strategic planning project can help get the whole process established.

Participatory strategic planning involves designing a series of task-force groups to develop a set of suggestions for taking the institution to a higher level of academic distinction. Some groups explore institution-wide issues, such as uses of technology, overall undergraduate experience, effectiveness of graduate programmes, community relationships, international programmes, and so forth. Others are formed around existing programmes and in essence spend their time doing a SWOT analysis – identifying strengths, weaknesses, opportunities and threats.

At the conclusion a report is written which becomes the basis for future programme enhancements and fundraising initiatives. But the major lasting effect from an integrated marketing point of view is that several hundred stakeholders and opinion leaders from inside and outside the institution have worked together and solidified relationships. Now the institution has a network of its most important supporters who feel involved and are ready to move the institution ahead.

Integrated marketing and the future of higher education ∎

The goals of integrated marketing are to mobilize everyone in an institution to help it advance and develop the kind of leadership necessary for participatory planning and implementation. Integrated marketing truly has the power to transform an institution's role in society and to make it more effective in an increasingly competitive marketplace. It seems, therefore, that this topic of the moment in the field of higher education could very well bring a permanent change to how colleges and universities in the future are planned and managed all over the world.

Further reading ∎

Beckworth, H. (1997) *Selling the Invisible*. New York: Warner Books.

Hayes, T. (1991) *New Strategies in Higher Education Marketing*. New York: The Hayworth Press.

Ind, N. (1997) *The Corporate Brand*. London: Macmillan.

Journal of Marketing for Higher Education (1989 to 1999).

Kotler, P. and Fox, K.F.A. (1985) *Strategic Marketing for Educational Institutions*. Englewood Cliffs, NJ: Prentice Hall.

Kotter, J.P. (1996) *Leading Change*. Cambridge, MA: Harvard Business School Press.

Lahey, A. (1999) Branding the academy, *University Affairs*, August/September.

Lauer, L.D. (1998) *Communication Power*. Gaithersburg, MD: Aspen.

Lauer, L.D. (1998) Need visibility: get integrated, *CASE Currents*, January: 12.

Lauer, L.D. (1999) Marketing across the board, *CASE Currents,* January: 18.

Lauer, L.D. (2000) Integrated marketing, *Advancement Handbook*, p.377. Washington DC: CASE Books.

Lauer, L.D. (2000) Participatory strategic planning, *CASE Currents*, April: 18.

McKenna, R. (1991) *Relationship Marketing*. Reading, MA: Addison-Wesley.

Moore, R. (1999) Surveying the field, *CASE Currents*, January: 26.

Proceedings of Symposium for the Marketing of Higher Education (1989 to 1999). Chicago: American Marketing Association.

Schultz, D., Tannenbaum, S. and Lauterborn, R.F. (1992) *Integrated Marketing Communications*. Chicago: NTC Business Books.

Senge, P.M. (1990) *The Fifth Discipline*. New York: Doubleday.

Sevier, R. (1998) *Integrated Marketing for Colleges, Universities and Schools*. Washington, DC: CASE Books.

Sevier, R. and Johnson, R. (1999) *Integrated Marketing Communication*. Washington, DC: CASE Books.

Simpson, C. (1998) The day we closed the news bureau, *CASE Currents*, January: 26.

Topor, R. (1983) *Marketing Higher Education*. Washington, DC: CASE Books.

Wang, P. and Petrison, L. (1992) Integrated marketing communications and its potential effects on media planning, *Journal of Media Planning*, Fall.

Wheatley, M. (1992) *Leadership and the New Science*. San Francisco: Berrett-Koehler.

Zyman, S. (1999) *The End of Marketing as We Know It*. New York: Harper-Business.

Peyronel has traversed some of this ground. He has argued that vice-chancellors and other senior administrators will seek the views of public affairs executives only 'if they are perceived as credible and informed advisors'.[2] He says that senior public affairs people are often 'pigeonholed' in the technical aspects of their jobs and find it difficult to play a meaningful role in institutional decision-making.[3] In dealing with the views which senior public affairs people and their chief executives have about the formers' role in institutions, he cites research which, not surprisingly, points to differences.[4] Peyronel concludes that public affairs directors must 'strive for a key role in institutional management and not allow themselves to be limited to the role of communication technician or information processor'.[5] Kinnick and Cameron report that the 'power-control perspective' of the dominant coalition in an organization is likely to resist changing the status quo in which senior public affairs managers are not at the decision-making table unless a compelling benefit is evident.[6]

But the issue has more to it than what some might describe as a lack of appreciation of the role of public affairs among senior management. Some of the failures to be heard at the top level have to do with the failure of individual public affairs executives to show their worth as both technician and counsellor. Woodrum describes an organization's chief executive as the 'principal client' of the public affairs executive[7] and the craft they practise as very *personal* business.[8] There is, Woodrum argues, no other staff position which requires such a personal relationship with the chief executive. He was writing about failure among senior public affairs directors in their special roles. However, his warnings that many are not delivering the product that the 'principal client' wants, and that they forget the reasons why they were employed in the first place, are appropriate ones for those public affairs practitioners yet to join the dominant coalition. In his list of eight attributes that chief executives desire in public relations executives, Woodrum includes: thinking like the chief executive and being 'interested in the business, enthusiastic about the company's prospects, and anxious to work and help achieve a new success' for the organization.[9] Moreover, such executives need to analyse every problem and opportunity as a businessperson.

Drobis has been far more direct in identifying what public affairs executives should do if they are yet to get a seat at the decision-making table. 'If a public relations professional isn't having impact on the organization's policy and performance, well, forgive my bluntness, but it's time to earn that responsibility or find a new job.'[10] He argues that one of the more fruitful approaches, and a higher valuation of the function overall, is immersion in the organization's strategic plan. This can be done not only by providing input to the development of the plan, but also by identifying plan objectives that public relations can help to achieve and being ready to have them evaluated.[11]

Such a view will have resonance for chief executives in higher education who increasingly reflect their business counterparts in demanding more of their senior public affairs staff. Much of this has to do with the pressures that constant change places on the universities. This change is driven by reductions in traditional sources of public income and the consequential need to diversify. This in turn generates pressures to delineate more clearly and aggressively to a discerning market the institution's comparative advantages.

Universities are increasingly accountable not only for the outcomes of their teaching and research, but for the way in which they seek, allocate and spend their money. The market, of course, has always held universities accountable for teaching and research outcomes. Publicity about bad student experiences, inadequate lecture theatres and poor equipment does not help to attract bright new students; no one wants to fund research programmes that do not produce, nor institutions that simply do not have the academic power to advance knowledge.

In Australia, for example, more than a decade of change has included a new competitive environment following the forced amalgamations of institutions, the creation in the late 1980s of 'new' universities from the old colleges of advanced education and, more recently, severe cuts to government funding. Even in this tough environment, the bureaucrats in government departments continue to seek more and more detailed information through form-filling, audits, surveys, profile discussions and quality assessments. This heavy bureaucratic demand moved one Australian vice-chancellor to comment: 'Universities [are] already accountable to the death in fiscal and managerial terms . . . quality audits [will] extend this to greater accountability to students.'[12]

As universities are made more accountable for less public funding, the internal search for cost-effectiveness and efficiency will focus inevitably on public relations.[13] This search will be driven by people whose natural affinity is with tidy balance sheets, not communications. The most important issue will be how to respond to the challenge of supporting the efforts of institutions in the increasingly competitive environment while budgets are more closely scrutinized, perhaps reduced. The solution is a creative programme that positions universities effectively in the market and in the debates that influence the policy settings in which universities operate. The problem will be finding ways to justify to vice-chancellors that public relations and all that goes with it actually delivers a direct, positive impact on the bottom line. The proposition that universities have no reason to have public relations units other than to support their student recruitment efforts and their quest for research funding is a reasonable starting point to convincing practitioners of the need to justify what they do. Student recruiters have an obvious bottom line performance indicator: enrolment.[14] In Australia, that means at least meeting government-imposed enrolment targets for domestic students. Full-fee paying international students, and, in some universities, full fees from domestic students,[15] provide a financial boost.

As universities refine their responses to these pressures, senior public affairs staff must have more than the standard professional skills set. To prove their value, they must communicate with the institution's senior executive in the executive's technical language: they must 'talk the talk'. They must understand the politics of the higher education sector and their institution's role in them to the same level as the executive; they must take opportunities to demonstrate their policy worth to an organization, as well as maintain their technical abilities. They need to demonstrate the compelling benefit that public affairs brings to the organization. A seat at the decision-making table will be offered only if performance meets expectations.

One way of demonstrating such a benefit is to prove it by reporting regularly on public affairs outcomes of a planned set of objectives linked to the institution's strategic plan. But public affairs staff need to stop talking about evaluation and do it.

In 1994, a survey in the United States, Australia and South Africa found that about 95 per cent of public relations practitioners agreed that evaluation was more talked about than done.[16] Most, on the other hand, believed evaluation was necessary.[17] The authors of the paper in which those results were quoted concluded that, without evaluation, proving the worth of public relations is difficult, accountability missing and professional and personal rewards constrained.[18] The reason the survey turned up these results is that the last step in the four-step public relations process of research, planning, implementation and evaluation, is not often well pursued. Evaluation is, after all, time consuming, especially when public affairs areas are under-resourced and must focus on coping with day-to-day reality. And it is not easy to devise a mechanism by which outcomes can be measured.

Tymson has argued that if public relations is to prove its value, behaviour must be measured. Public relations must be 'goal-oriented, planned, self-starting and measurable'.[19] Measurement, she writes, focuses on desired results, not activities.[20] Others argue that 'evaluation should be sufficient only to prove that activity is well directed, well implemented and achieving the desired result'.[21] In their discussion of a systems approach to the theoretical model for public relations, Cutlip and colleagues deal with these themes of behaviour and results. In their view, public relations efforts are part of an organization's purposive and, therefore, managed behaviour to achieve results. They argue that organizations must continually adjust their relationships with publics in response to ever-changing social milieux.[22] Hainsworth and Wilson argue that to ensure systematic and ongoing evaluation, such evaluation must be part of the programme plan and be undertaken immediately on implementation or as soon as is feasible.[23] Finally, there is a hard-line view of all this: if you cannot measure its results then cut it out of the budget.[24]

If public affairs is about influencing behaviour and adjusting relationships, such behavioural changes ought to be capable of measurement. If they can be measured, the results ought to be reported up the line. One way of addressing this issue is to construct an evaluation model which blends an approach to measuring results[25] with strategic public relations planning, and which shows a clear line between what public affairs does and the institution's strategic plan.

Volkmann links planning and evaluation in a quite direct way: you must know what you are going to do before you do it, and you must have the people and the ability to pull it off.[26] Knowing what is to be measured well before it is measured is the key to evaluation. Andrews[27] says evaluation models must:

- be rational, understandable and simple
- take into account the dilemma faced by the majority of public affairs[28] directors: that of having more responsibility than authority. Public affairs, Andrews argues, is 'far more dependent than most other functions on players not only outside its own offices but outside the company'[29]
- deal explicitly with the difficulty of knowing with confidence that there is a true cause and effect between action and result
- be flexible and recognize that the public affairs time horizon can range from a few days for a crisis to many years for an intractable issue

To devise the model, Andrews researched the efforts to which a number of key US companies went to find ways to judge the effectiveness of their public affairs offices. That research found that most public affairs programmes have three distinct categories of goals:

- to gain and maintain credibility and legitimacy
- to facilitate timely and appropriate responses
- to have a positive financial impact.

Andrews notes that all public affairs activities can be defined in terms of one or more of these comprehensive categories.

Being regarded as credible is vital for all organizations, especially those selling in the market or seeking to contribute to public policy debates. In 1995, the chief executive of General Motors put it this way when discussing the company's concerns with media reporting of a safety issue:

> We will not be silent when we have been wronged. We are asking for accountability and responsibility on the part of this media. We also recognise that this kind of demand places an equal responsibility on us to be candid and forthright.[30]

Media liaison is aimed primarily at generating the credibility a university or college seeks for itself and its academic staff. It seeks credibility so that it may recruit the best staff and students, influence debate about, say, increased research funding, and protect its intellectual property. Perhaps a media release from the vice-chancellor calling for an immediate 10 per cent increase in such funds was designed to contribute to a policy debate. Perhaps, also, it was aimed at convincing an internal audience of research-only academics that the vice-chancellor means to support them. Both goals enhance credibility. Media liaison also has a reactionary function – responding to journalists' requests for expert commentators, for example. Professional media staff try to respond to journalists as quickly as possible because they know the time pressures under which the media operate. It does not take long for the word to get about that the media staff at the University of Inconsequential Studies simply cannot respond in time, or they simply ignore journalists.

The model that Andrews developed[31] is easily linked to strategic public affairs planning. It has four basic steps.

- Decide precisely what is to be measured.
- Identify specific public affairs goals.
- Set out basic public affairs tasks (four categories).
- Measure the activities.

Too often the self-evident point that you need to decide precisely what is to be measured is overlooked, and success – or failure – is measured at the macro level rather than at the micro level, or people rather than programmes are evaluated. So the model provides a mechanism to help decide the level at which measurement is undertaken, based on the proposition that some activities are quite comprehensive, some less so. For clarity, this discussion of the model uses the categories of Programme, Component and Activity to describe the three levels of public affairs activity:[32]

Programme = the entire public affairs unit
Component = major groupings of functions within the unit
   Activity = micro-level activities such as VIP visits, the campus
             newspaper, media liaison

Evaluating one activity at a time, rather than the whole programme, makes it much easier to fit operations to the model.

Andrews' model sorts public affairs tasks into four categories:

- Intelligence gathering (which includes analysis, monitoring emerging issues, trend analysis).
- Internal coordination (includes liaison with planning people, developing issue position papers).
- External communications (media releases, campus newspaper, publications, experts list).
- Action programmes (lobbying, VIP visits, events).

The task categories are allied closely to the goals, and frequently overlap two or more goals. Andrews suggests developing a grid using the links between goals and task areas to guide the evaluation of activities. All three goals are important to each task, but not necessarily of equal importance. On the grid, the primary goal for each task area is indicated by an A, the secondary goals by a B. This approach can be modified to include the three goals under the heading 'key result areas' and by setting specific targets for each.[33]

Having established the model, link it to your strategic objectives and annual work programme by writing public relations plans that set specific goals, tasks and budgets for each activity in the overall programme. Link all you do to the objectives of the institution's strategic plan. Involve the entire public affairs staff in this task, for that will help them to understand more clearly where their special cog fits in the bigger wheel. Arranging the programme in this way not only provides a road map for where you and your staff are going, but also demonstrates to the 'principal client' and senior management group that you can measure public affairs, that you can demonstrate a bottom-line impact, and that your programme is delivering positive outcomes.

The annual assessment involves evaluating each task against its primary goal using a range of objective and subjective measures. Quantitative assessments are important, but there is nothing wrong with using qualitative measures as well.

Credibility and legitimacy are two important notions that together define an organization's reputation, or at least go a long way towards that. To be credible, an organization must be worthy of belief or of gaining and maintaining confidence[34] when it pronounces on an issue or, in the case of universities, seeks to enrol students: what we offer is what you get. A credibility gap is the difference between what is said and what is actually meant or done.[35] Legitimacy is about being lawful and genuine, not spurious;[36] indeed, about having a rightful place in the market or in a public debate. Thus demonstrating an organization's credibility and its legitimacy is probably the most important public affairs task. It is especially important that universities are recognized as credible and legitimate. This is not only to build and enhance a reputation as an excellent place to study or to research, but also to ensure that the claims made in recruitment slogans can be justified and to demonstrate to potential funding sources – government and private – that the institution is the place in which to invest research funds because it has a top-class reputation.

Andrews argued that all the methods of measuring performance in this key goal category are measures of how well an organization *influences* its target audiences. Andrews suggests criteria for judging how well an organization does in influencing credibility and legitimacy in each of its public affairs 'activities'. These are the four basic public relations steps: awareness, opinion, commitment and action. Influence exerted in each of the criteria ranges from negative to unsuccessful to maintained to expanded.[37] The tools which might be used to evaluate activities for success in this key goal include surveys, questionnaires, interviews, audits and statistical activity like attitude scaling and variance analysis.

The ability to respond in a timely way to crises, emerging issues, the newest twist in wage negotiations with unions, to provide the 'principal client' with urgent advice, or simply to produce an academic expert to comment on the latest political development, is crucial to the senior public affairs role. Success also has internal dimensions. When, for example, the institution expresses a view about declining government funding, or the need for new postdoctoral research fellowships, it demonstrates to staff that senior management does more than get in the way of progress. But a response capability includes anticipating issues and the manner in which they are handled.

Andrews' criteria for measuring response capability are: (1) scan and gather information, (2) analyse, (3) advise and counsel management, (4) determine courses of action, and (5) act.[38] Evaluating responses can be done on the basis of how issues are (a) mishandled, (b) missed, (c) anticipated, (d) handled, and/or (e) avoided. The quality, accuracy and speed of responses also need to be measured. Public affairs practitioners find financial performance a particularly difficult area. Student recruiters can show a numerical, thus bottom-line, impact from their efforts. But how can the public affairs staff show a bottom-line result? In the first place, they are a cost item on the budget,[39] so any effort to do the same with less (or more with the same) in tough financial times has an immediate bottom-line impact. It is clear that many public relations activities can be reviewed to generate savings, however much practitioners dislike having to do it. Simple steps, like finding an alternative to the public relations department's front counter selling tickets to functions, accepting sponsorship, or making sure that public relations professionals do not get involved in activity which is best done by others, are examples.

Research supports the view that public relations can actually generate revenue.[40] A survey of public relations practitioners in corporations in the *Fortune 500* list tested three hypotheses: (1) that increasing public relations expense will have a positive relationship effect on the company's reputation; (2) that improving the reputation of the company will have a positive relationship on the company's revenues; and (3) that increasing market share will have a positive relationship on the company's revenues. While the author cautions against generalizing the results for all US corporations, the data showed that when public relations expense increased in the sample companies, so, too, did their reputations.[41] The data also showed that about 7.6 per cent of reputation, and 53.4 per cent of revenue, could be explained by the statistical model developed to test the hypotheses.[42]

If the evaluation is to be taken seriously, negative results need to be included. How they are used depends on how the model has been adapted. For example, a quantitative measure about the accuracy of articles in the campus newspaper might be developed. This could include showing the number of complaints from academics and others. It might also include the frequency of typographical errors over time, and the number of research topics covered.

A range of quantitative measures, from surveys and frequency counts and statistical analyses, can be applied to the model. Identify and use those which work for the programme but, at the very least, find some which show progression against benchmarks, specific quarterly or annual goals, or met targets, including budgets, set at the beginning of the year. Similarly, the scope of qualitative measures allows plaudits from satisfied academics, a comment from a journalist, or a letter from a participant in an event to be used in the evaluation.

According to Woodrum, the major complaint and request of chief executives is the lack of positive media coverage and the desire for more of it.[43] That a vice-chancellor should want more and better media coverage in the tough competitive environment they face is hardly surprising. You may not be able to make it happen, but you can aim to achieve an increase and you can report on what is actually occurring now. If you find out the extent of the media's coverage of your institution, you may surprise yourself and delight your 'principal client'.

As Australia's only university specially funded for basic research, the Australian National University (ANU) has a vested interest in protecting its special status. One important element in this is its ability to generate positive media coverage, and Andrews' model has provided the mechanism by which this can be evaluated. Two *activities* in ANU's public affairs *program* are tasked to generate that coverage: the fortnightly newspaper, 'ANU Reporter', and media liaison. 'ANU Reporter' and media liaison are external communications activities under the basic tasks category; both have primary goals of enhancing the university's credibility and legitimacy. Media liaison has another primary goal of *response capability*. Both have secondary goals related to generating a *financial impact*. Mainstream media pick-up of 'ANU Reporter' research articles, the number and nature of enquiries from journalists, and the total mainstream media coverage of the university are tracked annually. A database enables continuing annual comparisons, provides information about whether coverage is positive, negative or neutral, and sorts coverage of research into discipline areas.

Tracking and reporting media coverage has demonstrated that research outcomes, either through media releases based on journal articles, or as a result of pick-up from 'ANU Reporter' stories, consistently dominate media interest in the university. This is an important *influence-enhancing* result for a university established specifically for research purposes and known internationally for its outcomes. It is a result directly sought by the important public affairs goal of 'promoting greater awareness and understanding of [the university's] achievements in research'[44]. It is also a defined key result expectation for gaining and maintaining credibility and legitimacy for the university through the media.[45]

In the second half of calendar 1999,[46] for example, 68 per cent of the 603 media enquiries handled by the media liaison office were about research topics. Only 3 per cent were about teaching. Of the 2689 references to the university recorded in the media monitored for the daily summary in 1999, 70 per cent were about ANU research. Only 2 per cent were about teaching. Enquiries from reporters seeking expert comments on issues of the day accounted for 69 per cent of total enquiries; 25 per cent of enquiries were generated by ANU media releases; and 6 per cent by 'ANU Reporter'. The remainder were stimulated by journal articles or other factors. While 60 per cent of media calls were for information to be included in news reports, 36 per cent were for academic analysis for comment pieces. Economic and political developments in Asia through 1999 accounted for 15 per cent of media enquiries during the second half of the year, and 11 per cent of the full year's media references to the university. This is a vital finding for a university that has world-leading expertise on all aspects of Asian society. Medical research generated 12 per cent of enquiries for the second half of the year and 11 per cent of full-year media references, a result directly linked to planned public relations activity to promote two research breakthroughs. Of the total recorded coverage of the university in the daily media monitoring service, 80 per cent resulted from enquiries, 14 per cent were generated by a media release, and 14 per cent resulted from an article published in 'ANU Reporter'. Only one edition of the 'ANU Reporter' in 1999 missed attracting some coverage. However, most stories picked up from the publication generated coverage in major daily newspapers or on radio and television.

Equally important is the extent of national coverage by the media. With a relatively small media sector, it is reasonably easy to identify such coverage in Australia. For ANU's assessment of such coverage, data were collected from the daily clipping service for the two national dailies, the two major capital city newspapers, and the daily newspaper in the national capital (where the university is located) which is read by politicians and senior bureaucrats. These newspapers in 1999 accounted for about 38 per cent of total newspaper coverage of the university. The 'local' daily did not account for the vast majority of newspaper coverage of ANU as had been expected by some in the dominant coalition. That place was held by one of the national dailies with its higher education supplement. Similarly, that paper had more references to ANU on page one than did the local. The extent to which major newspapers outside the national capital mentioned the university on page one and in early general news surprised everyone.

The data are also important simply because they exist. ANU now knows more about who covers it, what interests them and when they become interested. It is, frankly, important to be able to show the medical research school, which believes it does not receive sufficient media coverage, that when it does have real news this will be reported. It is equally important to be able to demonstrate that coverage of negative issues is overwhelmed by that of positive matters. This information is used to inform decisions about media targeting. An evaluation of this nature does not, of course, tell the university whether all the good news about research generates a positive perception among target audiences, or whether target audiences hold a negative view based on coverage of, for example, protracted industrial unrest. Fortunately, opinion research conducted in 1998 among potential and first-year students went part-way towards relieving this as a problem. It showed that the university's reputation among these groups on most areas of comparison with a set of other universities was excellent.

Perhaps more importantly, exposure of the media data to the 'principal client', the senior management and deans of faculties and directors of research schools led to a positive perception of the role of media relations in the public affairs operation. It dispelled misconceptions about performance and led to a request that reports should be produced more frequently.

Reporting the results of performance evaluations of public affairs programmes is an important step in generating access to the dominant coalition on a regular basis. Such reports demonstrate that funds committed to public affairs do generate anticipated outcomes and are therefore well spent. It is important that senior public affairs executives recognize that the power to get them a seat at the table is in their own hands. Woodrum argues that one of the fundamental attributes of public affairs executives who succeed is being results-oriented. They have to make something happen by doing something as simple as setting an objective and then achieving it.[47] As the sporting advertisement says, 'Just do it'.

Notes ◼

1 K.N. Kinnick and G.T. Cameron (1994) Teaching public relations management: the current state of the art, *Public Relations Review*, 20(1): 73–88.
2 A.C. Peyronel (2000) Higher education public relations at the year 2000: assessing the status of public relations at colleges and universities, *The CASE International Journal of Educational Advancement*, 1(1): 67–73.
3 Ibid., p.67.
4 Ibid., pp.69–70.
5 Ibid., p.71.
6 Kinnick and Cameron op.cit., p.75.
7 R.L. Woodrum (1995) How to please the CEO and keep your job, *The Public Relations Strategist*, 1(3): 7.
8 Ibid., p.9.
9 Ibid., pp.10–11.
10 D.R. Drobis (1966) Stop whining and take a seat!, *The Public Relations Strategist*, 2(1): 38.
11 Ibid., p.39
12 Professor B. Wilson (1993) quoted in S. Twist and F. Carruthers, Committee to sort the weak from the strong, *The Australian*, 30 June.

13 In our roles we work closely with alumni, development and student recruitment staffs. In many universities these are part of the same administrative organization, but not all university structures so combine these allied fields.

14 Enrolment is complicated by the desire of all universities in Australia to maintain entry standards. The universities set their own minimum entry standards, but, faced with high demand and a supply of places imposed by the government's target load for new-to-higher-education students, the margin can be pushed lower than most wish it to go.

15 From the 1998 academic year, Australian universities were permitted to admit domestic students on a full-fee paying basis provided the institutions had first met their new-to-higher-education target loads.

16 United States 94.3 per cent, Australia 95 per cent, South Africa 97.7 per cent. International Public Relations Association (1994) *Gold Public Relations Evaluation: Professional Accountability* Paper No. 11, p.4. Sydney: IPRA.

17 United States 75.9 per cent, Australia 90 per cent, South Africa 89.1 per cent. Ibid.

18 Ibid., p.37.

19 C. Tymson (1987) Measuring results, in R. Siedle (ed.) *Managing Public Relations in Australia*. Melbourne: Public Relations Institute of Australia, p.23.

20 Ibid., p.24.

21 International Public Relations Association op.cit., p.10.

22 S.M. Cutlip, A.H. Center, and G.M. Broom (1985) *Effective Public Relations*, 6th edn. Englewood Cliffs, NJ: Prentice Hall, p.185.

23 B.E. Hainsworth and L.J. Wilson (1992) Strategic program planning, *Public Relations Review*, 18(1): 14.

24 R. Siedle (1987) A model for public relations management in Australia, in Siedle op.cit., p.7.

25 P.N. Andrews (1985) The sticky wicket of evaluating public affairs: thoughts about a framework, *Public Affairs Review*. Washington, DC: Public Affairs Council, pp.94–105.

26 M.F. Volkmann (1994) Planning and organizing the public relations program for results. Paper presented at Australian Vice-Chancellors' Committee public relations conference, Adelaide, p.15.

27 Andrews op.cit, p.95.

28 While there is considerable debate about which of the terms public 'relations' and public 'affairs' is the correct descriptor for what we do (I prefer 'affairs' because it is more comprehensive), the terms are regarded as synonymous for the purposes of this chapter.

29 Andrews op.cit., p.95.

30 J.F. Smith quoted in L.G. Foster (1995) Ten CEOs send a message to public relations, *The Public Relations Strategist*, 1(1): 9.

31 For a detailed discussion about using the Andrews' model, see Mahoney (2000) Accountable to the death: a model for evaluating public relations, *The CASE International Journal of Educational Advancement*, 1(1): 40–52, from which this chapter is drawn.

32 Andrews uses the variation 'PROGRAM', 'Program', 'program' to describe the three levels of public affairs activity.

33 Similarly, we have used 'Programme', 'Components' and 'Activities' at a level below the divisional operation so that each of our major groupings of activities can be classified as a 'Programme'.

34 *The Macquarie Dictionary* (1985). Sydney: Macquarie Library Pty Ltd., p.433.

35 Ibid.

36 Ibid., p.991.

37 Andrews op.cit., p.99.

38 Ibid., p.101.

39 Ibid.

40 Y.W. Kim (1999) Measuring the bottom-line impact of public relations at the organizational level. Paper submitted to the Institute for Public Relations for the 1998 Smart Grant, Florida.

41 Ibid., p.20.

42 Ibid., p.21.

43 Woodrum op.cit., p.10.

44 Excerpt from the 'Media and information services' goal of the ANU Public Affairs Division's 1999 work plan. The plan's structure mirrors Andrews' evaluation model outline, p.4.

45 Ibid.

46 While the database records media references for the full calendar year, data about media enquiries are recorded for the second half only as a result of staffing changes.

47 Woodrum op.cit., p.11.

Appendix

THE UNIVERSITY OF BIRMINGHAM CODE OF PRACTICE: PUBLICATIONS AND COMMUNICATIONS

1 Preamble

It is part of the University's mission to publish and communicate the results of scholarship and research. It is its policy to present and promote itself consistently and vigorously as an institution committed to high quality in teaching, research and management. The purpose of this code of practice is to provide a framework within which those activities of publication and communication may be undertaken in ways which protect the interests of the University, its members and the principle of academic freedom.

2 Scope

This code is concerned with all forms of communication, including written, printed and electronic, by employees in their capacity as members of the University. For all such publications and communications the University, as either originating address or employer, may be held responsible in law either on its own or together with the author. For this reason the University has adopted this code of practice to regulate the issue of publications and communications for which it may be held responsible. Although the law makes no distinction, the University has chosen not to exercise formal institutional control over the publication or communication of academic work by members of its academic staff as part of its commitment to the principle of academic freedom. Therefore, although the University acknowledges and asserts its ultimate responsibility for all publications or communications by its staff in their professional capacity, the code is concerned with and confined to publications and communications which are made by the University as an institution or on its behalf by its members or which may appear to others to be so.

3 Editorial Responsibility

It is the responsibility of all members of the University to exercise judgement and care to ensure that publications and communications are not detrimental to the good name of the University and are consistent with this code of practice. It is for the individual to be aware of the levels of editorial control required by the University as described below and to make a judgement on the correct level, if any, appropriate to the work in hand. Authors should also have regard to any relevant provisions in their contract of employment.

4 Criteria for Deciding Levels of Editorial Control

The Content
Authors should take account of the degree to which the content of the communication or publication is important to the work or reputation of the University. The answer to the question: 'How damaging would it be to the interests of the University if this publication or communication were inaccurate or inconsistent with University policies?' will provide guidance.

Distribution/Access
Authors should consider the potential readership of the communication or publication based on: the number of copies to be printed; the potential number of readers per copy; the number of addressees of an electronic communication; the number of potential readers with access via a computer network. In general, the greater the number of potential readers, the higher the level of editorial control required.

Degree of Association with the University
Authors should consider the extent to which, by virtue of its content or appearance, the publication or communication will suggest to the reader that it emanates from and with the authority of the University. It should be assumed that disclaimers will not be effective in absolving the University of responsibility or in protecting its reputation.

5 Editorial Control

These are the levels of editorial control applicable to different communications and publications. Authors are responsible for ensuring that the appropriate level of authority is obtained for each communication or publication. In each category examples are given. Further advice is available from the External Relations and Development Office which is also responsible for making recommendations to the Vice-Chancellor in cases where the appropriate level is not evident from the provisions of this code.

Level 1

Full University Control
Publications and communications edited centrally by a responsible office, normally the External Relations and Development Office.

Examples:
- *Undergraduate Prospectus*
- *Postgraduate Prospectus*
- *The Bulletin*
- *The Birmingham Magazine*
- *Court Reporter*
- *Annual Report*
- *Annual Accounts*

and electronic equivalents including certain documents within the Campus Information Service.

Level 2

Review and Approval of Content by University
Publications and communications drafted within Schools or administrative offices but subject to central review before publication. The External Relations and Development Office has authority delegated from the Vice-Chancellor to give University approvals at this level following prior approval by the Head of Budget Centre.

Examples:
- Any promotional material in any medium produced for the recruitment of students, postgraduate, undergraduate, occasional, etc, including general leaflets, exhibitions, advertisements, brochures.
- Material promoting or advertising commercial services.
- Communications intended for the news media (other than letters for publication written by members of staff on subjects within their academic expertise).
- Statements within other publications which describe the University, its attributes and characteristics in a general way.
- General communications with alumni.
- Staff recruitment literature and advertisements.
- Fundraising material.
- Advertising by external organisations in University publications.
- Publications: *Report of Research and Publications, Calendar and Directory*.

Level 3

Review of Content and Approval by Head of Budget Centre
Material concerned only with one Budget Centre, other than material appropriate to Level 2.

Examples:
- Internal newsletters.
- Descriptive summaries of research work.
- Library catalogues.

Level 4

Self Approval
Communications or publications concerned only with an individual's professional or academic interest and expertise.

6 Management Information
The publication or communication of any University management information is subject to prior approval by the Registrar and Secretary, who may, in certain circumstances, elect to grant general approval for categories of information.

7 Corporate Identity Policy
Any material published or communicated bearing the name of the University is subject to the provisions of the University's corporate identity policy which includes requirements on design, typography and production standards. Advice is available from the External Relations and Development Office, which has authority delegated from the Vice-Chancellor to implement the policy.

8 Legal Consequences
Authors should exercise great care in publishing or communicating confidential information including personnel records and references. The sending by mail of material which is defamatory or breaches confidentiality or copyright or is obscene or in some other way contravenes the law can be more dangerous still if fax or electronic mail is used. Anyone concerned with a specific problem in these areas is invited to seek advice from the University's Legal Office before the communication is made.

Members of the University should have regard to the provisions of relevant legislation. This currently (November 1994) includes topics related to: copyright; libel; computer misuse; data protection; race relations; equal opportunities; official secrets; intellectual property; obscene publications; the protection of minors. Advice on these matters is available from the University's Legal Office.

Approved by the University Council on 21 December 1994.
© The University of Birmingham

INDEX

academic reticence, and research
  reputations, 3–4
academic staff
  and the Internet, 62–3, 64
  and the media, 66–7
  and the writing of prospectuses,
    40
academic standards
  maintaining, 20
  undergraduate prospectuses and
    images of, 37
accountability
  and external relations activities,
    1, 2
  and fundraising, 118–19
  of universities and public
    relations, 145–6
action programmes, 149
advertising, 44–54, 126
  achieving value for money, 52–3
  agencies, 47, 52–3
  budget, 44, 51–2
  effective, 46–7
  and integrated marketing, 139
  and lifestyle images, 46
  logos and positioning statements
    on advertisements, 8
  and marketing plans, 44–5, 53
  media selection, 51
  in newspapers, 46, 49, 52
  planning a campaign, 49–51

pressurized sales, 44
publications, 46–7
reaching target audiences, 45–7,
    48, 50, 51
role of research in, 47–9
  after the campaign, 49
  during the campaign, 49
  pre-campaign, 48
strategic approach to, 53–4
television, 46, 48, 49, 51
uniform approach to, 53
and visual identity, 17
advocacy polls, 22
agencies
  advertising, 47, 52–3
  and media interviews, 75
AlphaGalileo, 75
alumni relations, 3, 10, 97–107,
    125–6
  budgeting for, 99
  building a programme, 99
  careers and professional
    development, 106
  clubs
    geographic alumni, 102–3
    special-interest, 103–4
    starting, 104–5
  communications, 100–1
  and fundraising, 114, 116, 125,
    126
  future of, 107

importance of, 97–8
and integrated marketing, 131,
    138–9, 140
and the Internet, 57, 58, 60,
    64–5
e-students, 107
at the LSE, 98–9
and market research, 22, 28–9
on-campus events, 101–2
organization of, 99
performance measurements of,
    107
records (database), 100
reunions, 92, 93
service provision, 105–6
and student recruitment, 107,
    125
and student societies, 106–7
and the World Wide Web,
    100–1
Andrews, P.N., 147–8, 149, 150,
    152
anecdotes, in media interviews,
    73–4
anthropomorphism, in media
    interviews, 72–3
Apollo 13 (film), 68
Australian universities
    accountability of, 145
    Australian National University
        (ANU), 152
    enrolment targets, 146

benefits of effective external
    relations, 2–3
Birmingham University
    alumni magazine, 121–2
    centenary celebrations, 89
    code of practice on publications
        and communications, 127–8,
        157–60
    consultations with stakeholders,
        4
    examples of market research,
        21–2
    research on internal
        communication at, 79–82
    undergraduate prospectus, 35–7

brand positioning, and visual
    identity, 10
brand strategy development, 10,
    10–19
    arguments against adopting a
        brand strategy, 11–15
    and corporate identity, 13–14
    and corporate position, 12
    and diverse target audiences,
        11–12
    introducing a new visual identity,
        15–19
    and market position, 12–13
branding, and integrated marketing,
    135–6
brands, and the Internet, 60
Brannan, T., 44, 45, 46, 50
Branson, Sir Richard, 12
budgets
    advertising, 44, 51–2
    departmental, 7
    event management, 92
buildings, and corporate identity, 14

California, University of, 122
Cambridge University, and
    fundraising, 108
Cameron, G.T., 144
careers, and alumni relations, 106
CASE (Council for the
    Advancement and Support of
    Education), 118, 121, 122
Cassini-Huygens mission, 74
change, and visual identity, 16
charitable trusts and foundations,
    as potential donors, 113
chief executives, and public
    relations executives, 144–5
circulars, and internal
    communications, 80, 81, 82
committee meetings, and internal
    communications, 81, 82, 83,
    84
communication
    external communications, 149
    materials, and corporate identity,
        14
    see also internal communications

companies, as potential donors, 113
comparisons, in media interviews, 73
complex corporations, and corporate identity, 14
computers, and visual identity, 17, 18
conferences, 88
  market research on facilities for, 22
core values of brands, 13
corporate identity, and brand strategy development, 13–14, 19
corporate planning, and the marketing plan, 44–5
corporate positioning, and brand strategy development, 12, 19
Corstjens, J., 50
Council for the Advancement and Support of Education, *see* CASE
credibility
  and media coverage, 152
  and performance measurement, 150
credit card transactions, and e-commerce, 62
customer satisfaction, 6
Cutlip, S.M., 147

Data Protection Act, 94
Davies, Hunter, 'Born 1900' (article in 'The Birmingham Magazine'), 121–2
Delaware University, web-enabled campus, 60–1
departmental budgets, 7
design consultants, and visual identity planning, 15, 16–18
desk research, 48
digital printing, 42
direct mail, 45
Drobis, D.R., 144

e-commerce, 62
email, 63

employees
  attitudes of to organization leaders, 77
  importance to organizations of, 77, 78
European Union, legal requirements for publications, 42
evaluation, and performance measurement, 146–7
event management, 87–96
  alumni events, 101–2
  alumni reunions, 92, 93, 101
  basic questions about events, 88–9
  benefits of events, 87–8
  and Birmingham University centenary celebrations, 89
  budgeting, 92
  checklist, 95–6
  low reputation of, 88
  music, 91
  in other countries, 93
  partners' attendance at events, 94–5
  planning and briefing, 90–2
  publicity, 96
  royal visits, 92–2
  scope of events, 88
  staffing, 89–90
  structure and presentation, 95
  and team spirit, 96
  and VIPs, 93–4
events listings, 35
exhibitions, and visual identity, 17
external communications, 149
external customer satisfaction, 6

face-to-face interviews
  as a form of communication, 34
  in market research, 24
  media, 70
face-to-face meetings, and fundraising, 115–16
feasibility studies for fundraising, 110, 120
Feynman, Richard, 73

fundraising, 2, 3, 108–20
accountability, 118–19
and alumni relations, 114, 116,
125, 126
budgets, 118
campaigns, 108
development office, 117–18
feasibility studies, 110, 120
financing context of the
campaign, 111–12
finding potential donors, 112–16
gift tables, 112–13
telephone campaigns, 116
identifying and prioritizing needs,
110–11
and information officers, 123–4
and integrated marketing, 129,
140
internal campaign management
committees, 111
marketing plans, 119
planning and preparation, 108–
10, 109–19, 120
private phase of the campaign,
119
staff, 117, 118, 119
strategy, 115–16
volunteers' involvement in, 116

General Motors, 148
geographic alumni clubs, 102–3
Giddens, Anthony, 97, 98
gift tables, 112–13
grapevine/rumours, and internal
communications, 80, 81, 82
graphic design, 40–1, 126
internal services, 41
Greenall, John, 124, 125, 126

Hainsworth, B.E., 147
HEERA (Higher Education External
Relations Association), 122,
124
higher education
examples of research in, 21–2
maintaining standards of entry
to, 20
and the publications culture, 34

Higher Education External Relations
Association (HEERA), 122
humour, in media interviews, 74

ICFM (Institute of Charity
Fundraising Managers), 118
information officers
and fundraising, 123–4
and student power, 122–3
information technology staff, and
websites, 64
Institute of Charity Fundraising
Managers (ICFM), 118
integrated marketing, 79, 125,
129–41
and advertising, 139
and alumni, 131, 138–9, 140
and branding, 135–6
and communications, 130, 134–5
and development programmes,
140
and fundraising, 129, 140
and the future of higher
education, 141
launching, 137
and organizational goals, 130
and partnerships, 139–40
and place, 133–4
and price, 133
and product, 132–3
reasons for implementing, 129
and research, 136–7
and strategic planning, 140–1
and student recruitment, 129,
133–4, 138
taskforce, 137
at Texas Christian University,
131, 139
transforming institutions
through, 131–2
and visibility, 138–40
as a way of thinking, 130
intelligence gathering, 149
internal communications, 76–86
attitudes to central management,
80
breakdowns in, 76
circulars, 80, 81, 82

committee meetings, 81, 82, 83, 84
the grapevine/rumour, 80, 81, 82
and immediate bosses, 81, 82, 83, 84
local newspapers and radio, 81, 82
memoranda, 80, 81, 82
newsletters, 80, 81, 82, 83
noticeboards, 81, 82
in the private sector, 76–9
research at Birmingham University, 79–82
team briefings, 81, 82, 83, 84–5
trade unions, 81, 82
videos, 83–4
and the World Wide Web, 85–6
internal coordination, 149
internal customer satisfaction, 6
Internet, 55–65
and AlphaGalileo, 75
and alumni, 57, 58, 60, 64–5, 107
and Birmingham University, code of practice on publications and communications, 127–8
and business processes, 60–1
and e-commerce, 62
email, 63
as a form of communication, 33
and the future of residential-based education, 134
and integrated marketing, 139
learning and teaching, 62–3
and the promotion of a culture of change, 57–8
relations to other communications, 55–7
and staff training and development, 58
and student recruitment, 57
surveys, 23–4
use in the United States, 56–7
see also websites
interviews
market research, 23, 24
media, 66–75
agencies for, 75
anecdotes in, 73–4

answering questions, 70
anthropomorphism in, 72–3
comparisons in, 73
discussion format, 69–70
face-to-face, 70
humour in, 74
jargon or technicalities in, 71
live, 69
and the marketplace, 67–8
and misrepresentation, 66–7, 74
number problems in, 71
pre-recorded, 69
preparing for, 69–70
selecting material for, 70–1
similes in, 73
tone and style in, 72
interviews (market research)
face-to-face, 24
in-depth, 25
intranets
campus, 59, 60
and logos, 18

Jeans, James, *The Mysterious Universe*, 73
Jefkins, F., 47

Keen, Clive, 124, 125, 126
King's College London, 122
Kinnick, K.N., 144

Lauer, Larry, 125
learning, and the Internet, 62–3
legitimacy
and media coverage, 152
and performance measurement, 150
Levi, Primo, 73
lifestyle images, and advertising, 46
local radio
advertising on, 46–7
and internal communications, 81, 82
interviews on, 66–7
Lodge, David, *Nice Work*, 22
logos, 8–9, 15, 18, 19, 136

LSE (London School of Economics) and alumni relations, 98–9
 age of alumni, 107
 mission statement, 98
 special-interest clubs, 103

magazines, alumni, 100, 121–2
Making the Right Choice, 48
market position, and brand strategy development, 12–13
market research, 2, 6, 20–1
 in advertising, 47–9
 advocacy polls, 22
 agencies, 27, 31–2
 on alumni, 22, 28–9
 balancing costs and benefits of, 21, 30
 choosing the best technique, 26–7
 cost-effectiveness of, 31–2
 'deliverables', 31
 examples of higher education research, 21–2
 how it works, 22–3
 on internal communications at Birmingham University, 79–82
 primary data collection, 23–4
  face-to-face, 24
  self-completion, 23–4
  telephone surveys, 24
 and publications, 22, 35
 qualitative, 25–6
  when to use, 26–7
 quantitative, 23–4
  when to use, 27
 questions to ask, 30–1, 32
 role of opinion research, 20–1
 sampling, 27–30
  size of sample, 29–30
 secondary, 23
market segmentation
 and branding, 135–6
 and research, 136
marketing
 and publications, 126
 see also integrated marketing
Marketing and Communication Agency, 77

marketing plans, and fundraising, 119
marketing staff, and web-based services, 64
marketplace
 and the media, 67–8
 and university accountability, 145
Massachusetts University (Amherst), unofficial logos, 15
measurable outputs, 6
measurement, 2–3
Medawar, Peter, 72–3
media
 coverage, 151–4
 and individual staff members, 127
 and integrated marketing, 135
 and internal communications, 83
 liaison, 148, 152
 press officers, 126–7
 and royal visits, 93
 and student power, 122–3
media interviews, 66–75
 agencies for, 75
 anecdotes in, 73–4
 answering questions, 70
 and anthropomorphism, 72–3
 comparisons in, 73
 face-to-face, 70
 humour in, 74
 jargon or technicalities in, 71
 live, 69
 and the marketplace, 67–8
 metaphors in, 73
 and misrepresentation, 66–7, 74
 number problems in, 71
 pre-recorded, 69
 preparing for, 69–70
 selecting material for, 70–1
 similes in, 73
 tone and style in, 72
medical schools, assessing value of to local communities, 22
memoranda, and internal communications, 80, 81, 82

metaphors, in media interviews, 73
misrepresentation, and media interviews, 66-7, 74
mission and policies, 6
mission statements, 10, 79
  LSE Alumni Relations, 98
  market research on, 22, 26
MORI opinion polls
  on the Birmingham University undergraduate prospectus, 37
  face-to-face interviews, 24
  representativeness of, 30
  website, 23
music at events, 91
Muslim countries, event management in, 93

names, importance of, 8
newsletters
  alumni, 100
  and internal communications, 80, 81, 82, 83
newspaper advertising, 46, 49, 52
noticeboards, and internal communications, 81, 82

Ogilvy, David, 47, 48, 50
Oldham, Marie, 10, 11, 12
Olins, W., 13-14, 14
Omnibus surveys, 24
open days, 38, 88, 96
open-ended questions, in market research, 24, 31
opinion leaders
  and integrated marketing, 138
  market research on, 22
opinion research
  and students, 20-1, 154
  and visual identity, 15
  see also also market research
organizational structure, 121-8
  appointment of head of external relations, 124
  and the head of the institution, 125
  and information officers, 123-4
  and media relations, 126-7

organizations
  and corporate identity, 13-14
  reasons for external relations activities, 1-2
Oxford University, and fundraising, 108

part-time courses
  effective advertising of, 46-7
  postgraduate, 21
partnerships, and integrated marketing, 139-40
performance measurement, 143-54
  and accountability, 145-6
  of alumni relations, 107
  credibility and legitimacy, 150
  and evaluation, 146-7
  and media coverage, 151-4
  response capability, 150-1
  and strategic planning, 148-9
Peyronel, A.C., 144
place, and integrated marketing, 133-4
police, and event management, 93
policy decisions, and public relations outcomes, 143
positioning, and brand strategy development, 10, 11, 19
postal surveys, 23
postgraduate courses, part-time, 21
postgraduate prospectuses, 34
press advertising, 46, 49, 52
press releases, and product launch, 45
price, and integrated marketing, 133
printed material, importance of, 34
printing publications, 42
private sector, and internal communications, 76-9
product
  and corporate identity, 14
  and integrated marketing, 132-3
product launch, activities involved in, 45
product truth, 10, 11
professional associations, as potential donors, 113

professional development, and
alumni relations, 106
promotion, and integrated
marketing, 134
prospectuses
CD-ROM versions of, 21
market research on, 21, 25, 26
postgraduate, 34
writing, 39–40
see also undergraduate
prospectuses
public opinion
on higher education courses, 21
on the image of different
universities, 22
public relations (PR)
definition of, 3
executives as managers and
expert counsel, 143–5
and product launch, 45
reputation of, 1, 3
staff, 122
publications, 10, 33–43
and communication, 43
copywriting, 39–40
design, 40–1
distribution of, 42–3
editorial boards, 39
editors, 38–9
effective advertising of, 46–7
European Union legal
requirements for, 42
events listings, 35
and graphic design, 40–1, 126
illustrations, 41
and the importance of print, 34
internal newsletters, 80, 81, 82,
83
and the Internet, 33
and market research, 22, 35
and marketing, 126
and new media, 33–4
and organizational structure, 126
printing, 42
proof reading, 42
researching target audiences, 43
spending money on, 38
syllabuses, 35

and visual identity, 17
see also prospectuses

qualitative research, 25–6
when to use, 26–7
quality of product, and integrated
marketing, 132–3
quantitative research, 23–4
when to use, 27
questions, in media interviews, 70

radio advertising, 46–7
Red Cross, 57
reflexivity, in media interviews, 74
relationship marketing, and the
Internet, 65
reporting, between the community
and the higher education
institution, 5
reputation
of an organization, 150
of event management, 88
of public relations, 1, 3
research
and integrated marketing, 136–7
reputation, and external relations
activities, 3
residential campuses, and the
Internet, 134
response capability
measuring, 150–1
and media liaison, 152
revenue, generated by public
relations, 151
royal visits, 92

sales promotion, and product
launch, 45
sampling, 27–30
representative samples, 30
size of sample, 29–30
selection process (universities),
market research on, 21, 25,
27–8
seminars, 88
and product launch, 45
service organizations, and corporate
identity, 14

similes, in media interviews, 73
sixth-form students, market
    research on, 25, 27–8, 31
small companies, and corporate
    identity, 14
staff
    and event management, 89–90
    external relations professionals,
        122–5, 126–8
    fundraising, 117, 118, 119
    information technology, and
        websites, 64
    and internal communications
        at Birmingham University, 79
        importance of, 77
    motivation, 2
    recruitment, 2
    training and development, 58
    see also academic staff
stakeholders
    communications with, 1–2
    and integrated marketing, 129,
        138
    and market research, 32
stationery, and visual identity, 17
strategic approach to external
    relations, 4, 5–7
strategic planning
    and integrated marketing, 140–1
    and performance measurement,
        148–9
    and public relations executives,
        144–5
student accommodation, market
    research on, 21, 22, 31
student focus groups
    and advertising campaigns, 48
    and the Birmingham University
        undergraduate prospectus,
        36–7
student power, and the media,
    122–3
student recruitment
    and alumni relations, 107, 125
    and effective advertising, 46
    and external relations activities, 2
    and integrated marketing, 129,
        133–4, 138

and the Internet, 57
market research on, 21
and performance indicators, 146
    measuring response capabilities,
        151
student societies, and alumni
    relations, 106–7
students
    as helpers at events, 96
    and opinion research, 20–1, 154
SWOT analysis, and integrated
    marketing, 141
syllabuses, 35
systems of external relations, 5

target audiences, and brand strategy
    development, 11–12
teaching, and the Internet, 62–3
team briefings, and internal
    communications, 81, 82, 83,
        84–5
team spirit, and event management,
    96
team-building, and integrated
    marketing, 131–2
telephone calls, to prospective
    donors, 116
telephone interviews
    in market research, 24
    media, 70
Teletext, 52
television advertising, 46, 48, 49, 51
Texas Christian University (TCU),
    integrated marketing at, 131,
        139
top-down management, and the
    Internet, 58
trade unions, and internal
    communications, 81, 82

UMIST (University of Manchester
    Institute of Science and
    Technology), 122
undergraduate prospectuses, 34,
    35–8
    American model ('view book'),
        37–8
    balance of information, 36

cover, 36–7
design, 36–7
importance of, 35
information to include, 35–6
pictures, 36
United States
alumni communications, 100, 101
fundraising activities, 118
Internet use, 56–7
web-enabled campuses, 60–1
Universitas 21, 10
universities
identifying differences between, 4
student power and information
officers, 122–3
Universities UK (formerly the
Committee of Vice-
Chancellors and Principals),
75
university logos, 9

vice-chancellors
justifying public relations to,
145–6
and media coverage, 151–2
and public relations executives,
144
videos
as a form of communication,
33–4, 83–4
market research on designing, 21
and product launch, 45
VIPs, and event management, 93–4
Virgin, 12
visual identities, 8–19
and brand positioning, 10
and brand strategy development,
10–19
and graphic design, 41
and individual units, 18–19

introducing new, 15–19
look and feel, 16–17
making it happen, 18–19
making it work in practice,
17–18
what do we want to say?,
15–16
logos, 8–9, 15, 18, 19, 136
policing of, 125
Volkmann, M.F., 147
volunteers
and alumni clubs, 104–5
and fundraising, 116

web-enabled campus, at Delaware
University, 60–1
websites, 10
and advertising, 54
and alumni relations, 100–1
and internal communications,
85–6
market research on, 21, 25
for marketing higher education
institutions, 59–60
MORI, 23
and publications
internal, 35
postgraduate prospectuses, 34
strategies for effective use, 63–5
Westminster University, 122
Wilson, L.J., 147
Woodrum, R.L., 144, 151, 154
World Wide Web, *see* websites

young companies, and corporate
identity, 14
young people, and Internet use in
the United States, 56

Zarnecki, John, 74